Primary Teachers' Stress

Occupational stress is a global phenomenon. It is particularly acute in 'caring' occupations, such as teaching, where the restructuring of schools over the past decade has been accompanied by an escalation of teacher stress and burnout. The numbers leaving teaching have increased dramatically, while amongst those remaining in the profession, morale and levels of job satisfaction are low.

This book traces the sources of stress in teaching including:

- the effects of national policy;
- changes in work and school organisation;
- personal factors.

The authors explore teachers' perceptions of the causes of their stress, the experience and effects of stress, and the process of recovery and self-renewal. The book is based on interviews with primary school teachers clinically diagnosed as suffering from stress-related illness. These interviews are complemented by an organisational study of two primary schools, one a 'low' stress school, the other a 'high' stress school.

The findings inform policy recommendations aimed at preventing at source occupational stress in teaching and other 'caring' professions, as well as offering advice to individuals suffering from stress.

Geoff Troman is a Research Fellow and Associate Lecturer in the School of Education at the Open University.

Peter Woods is Professor of Education in the School of Education at the Open University, and a Research Professor in the Rolle School of Education at the University of Plymouth.

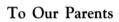

To Our Parents

Primary Teachers' Stress

Geoff Troman and Peter Woods

London and New York

First published 2001 by
RoutledgeFalmer
11 New Fetter Lane, London EC4P 4EE

Simultaneously published in the USA and Canada
by RoutledgeFalmer
29 West 35th Street, New York, NY 10001

RoutledgeFalmer is an imprint of the Taylor & Francis Group

© 2001 Geoff Troman and Peter Woods

Typeset in Goudy by
Florence Production Ltd, Stoodleigh, Devon
Printed and bound in Great Britain by
Biddles Ltd, Guildford and King's Lynn

British Library Cataloguing in Publication Data
A catalogue record for this book is available from the British Library

Library of Congress Cataloging in Publication Data
Primary teachers' stress/Geoff Troman and Peter Woods.
    p. cm.
  Includes bibliographical references and indexes.
  1. Elementary school teachers—Job stress—Great Britain.
  2. Burn out (Psychology).   3. Educational surveys—Great
Britain.   I. Troman, Geoff, 1946–.   II. Woods, Peter, 1934–.
LB2840.2 .P75 2001
372.11'001'9—dc21   00-059235

ISBN 0-415-22411-X (hbk)
ISBN 0-415-22412-8 (pbk)

Contents

Tables

Acknowledgements

There are many people without whose support our research and this resulting book would not have been possible. Most especially, we would like to thank the teachers who made up our core sample for their co-operation and for giving their time to disclose their very often painful reflections on their experiences in teaching, and how their work was impacting negatively on their physical, psychological and emotional health. Many were extremely ill throughout the research period as well as facing turmoil in their professional and personal lives. Their allowing us to share this phase in their lives attests to their commitment to both education and the teaching profession. We are proud to have been associated with them and feel privileged to tell their stories of self, work and social change. We are extremely grateful to the headteachers and teachers of the case study schools for their hospitality and generous allocation of time to the project. Their help and co-operation contributed greatly to our understanding of teachers' work. The assistance of the personnel department and the help and support of the occupational health manager and her secretary in the LEA where much of the research took place was invaluable. Our thanks also to an education officer in the LEA of one of our research schools for enabling access.

Thanks are due to members of our research team, Bob Jeffrey and Denise Carlyle, and thanks for their informed contributions to our regular discussions on teachers' work and stress. Thanks also to Martyn Hammersley and Andy Hargreaves for reading and making incisive comments on earlier drafts of some of the chapters. We must record here our thanks to the National Association of Schoolmasters and Union of Women Teachers, the National Union of Teachers, and the Professional Association of Teachers, for their help and advice in the early stages of the research. Also to Aileen Cousins who gave us valuable secretarial support, and Caroline Raine for her painstaking transcription of interview tapes. Special thanks are due to Maria for her unstinting and constant encouragement and practical, intellectual and emotional support throughout.

The research on which this book is based was funded by the Economic and Social Research Council (Award Number R000237166) and the Centre for Sociology and Social Research at the School of Education, The Open University, whose support is gratefully acknowledged.

A version of Chapter 1 was published as 'Teacher Stress in the Low-Trust Society' by the *British Journal of Sociology of Education*, 21(3) (2000) and we thank the editors at Taylor & Francis (PO Box 25, Abingdon, Oxfordshire, OX14 3UE) for permission to use the material here. An earlier version of Chapter 4 was published as 'Careers Under Stress: Teacher Adaptations at a Time of Intensive Reform' in the *Journal of Educational Change*, 1(3) (2000). It is used here by kind permission of Kluwer Academic Publishers. Earlier versions of chapters were presented as papers at: the *British Educational Research Association* Conferences, at University of Sussex, 1999 (Chapter 2) and University of Cardiff, 2000 (Chapter 4); and at the *European Educational Research Association* Conference, University of Edinburgh, 2000 (Chapter 6). We are grateful for the comments of participants at these conferences in developing our ideas.

Abbreviations

ATL	Association of Teachers and Lecturers
CACE	Central Advisory Council for Education
CEO	Chief Education Officer
DES	Department of Education and Science
DfEE	Department for Education and Employment
EBD	Emotional and Behavioural Difficulties
ERA	Education Reform Act
GP	General Practitioner
GTC	General Teaching Council
HEADLAMP	Headteacher Leadership and Management Programme
HMI	Her Majesty's Inspector
HSE	Health and Safety Executive
ILO	International Labour Office
IT	Information Technology
KS	Key Stage
LEA	Local Education Authority
LSA	Learning Support Assistant
NPQH	National Professional Qualification for Headship
NQT	Newly Qualified Teacher
Ofsted	Office for Standards in Education
Ofstin	Office for Standards in Inspection
PE	Physical Education
PTA	Parent Teacher Association
SAT	Standard Assessment Task
SEN	Special Educational Needs
UK	United Kingdom
USA	United States of America

Introduction

The growing incidence of teacher stress

Stress is a pervasive feature of contemporary life. The extent of occupational stress and stress-related illness, particularly in Western societies, is now well documented by social research (Newton et al., 1995; Bartlett, 1998). In the UK it is estimated that each working day 270,000 people are absent from work with stress, and in 1996 sickness absence cost UK businesses £12 billion (Ameghino, 1998). The HSE report that almost twenty million working days a year are lost because of work-related illness and, of the two million sufferers of job-linked illnesses, 500,000 workers say that stress is so bad that it is making them ill (Milne, 1998). The Teachers' Benevolent Fund has financed and organised a telephone helpline for stressed teachers (Nash, 2000). The government is particularly interested in teacher sickness and absence rates (Revell, 2000). This is evident in the Cabinet Office inquiry (1998) into 'Managing Attendance in the Public Sector' and by research areas prioritised by the DfEE (*Education Journal*, 1999: 31), for example, 'Ill health retirement and absenteeism amongst teachers'. The DfEE figures for England and Wales reported by Woodward (2000) claim 2.5 million working days were lost in 1999 at a cost of £3 million. The average teacher took nine days off. Of the 60 per cent of full-time teachers taking sick leave 44 per cent were absences of twenty days or more. The Education Secretary has committed himself to achieving the target of a 30 per cent fall in teachers' sick leave by 2002 (ibid.). Accompanying these trends has been a 90 per cent rise in mental health insurance claims in the years since 1994 (ibid.). The annual cost of stress to the Education Service in 1998 in England and Wales has been estimated at £230 million (Brown and Ralph, 1998).

Stress is a problem amongst the caring professionals generally and it has, for some time, been of particular concern in the teaching profession (Kyriacou and Sutcliffe, 1979; Kyriacou, 1980a). In the Dutch context, De Heus and Diekstra (1999) argue that teachers (particularly males) are more prone to stress and burnout than other professionals. Life insurance companies' actuaries claim that teachers are a high risk for sickness insurance as they are prone to stress-related illnesses and the burnout rate is high (Fisher, 1996). In the UK, a recent study of teachers' job satisfaction revealed 'unhappiness' being experienced amongst them (Gardner and Oswald, 1999). The authors state that while teachers are not the 'unhappiest workers' in the UK they are 'low by public sector standards compared especially to nurses'. This large-scale survey data indicated that the 'dissatisfiers' of teaching may be outweighing the 'satisfiers' (Nias, 1989). There is now a considerable international body of work which links teacher stress with the wholesale restructuring of national education systems, which began in the 1980s (Dunham, 1984; Travers and Cooper, 1996; Dinham and Scott, 1996; Woods et al., 1997; Brown and Ralph, 1998). For, since this time, the nature and demands of teaching have changed resulting in the intensification of teachers' work (Apple, 1986; Densmore, 1987; Campbell and Neill, 1994; Hargreaves, 1994; Woods, 1995a and b). Apple (1986) argues that, in modern capitalist societies, work intensifies as capital experiences an accumulation crisis and pressure for efficiency mounts in public and private sectors. Intensification leads to reduced time for relaxation and reskilling; causes chronic and persistent work overload; reduces quality of service; and separates the conceptualisation from the execution of tasks, making teachers dependent on outside expertise and reducing them to technicians (also see Hargreaves, 1994: 118–19).

Helsby (1999: 100) notes that: ' In a survey of over forty countries in 1991 the International Labour Office (ILO, 1991) found most teachers were experiencing stress and time pressures and that their overall workloads had increased, particularly in terms of new administrative duties and the time needed to deal with unruly students.' This supports research findings in Europe (Vandenberghe and Huberman, 1999), North America (Leithwood et al., 1999; and Smylie, 1999), and in Australia (Dinham, 1992; Dinham and Scott, 1996). In England and Wales 'heavy duty' accountability systems fuel the intensification of teachers' work and provide a major source of stress (Jeffrey and Woods, 1998; Helsby, 1999; Scanlon, 1999).

In our own recent researches (Woods, 1995a and b; Woods and Jeffrey, 1996; Woods et al., 1997), it is clear that stress is a major feature in the lives of teachers involved. Further, these stress levels, judging from our research and national figures, appear to be increasing. This is evident from the number of teachers retiring early owing to stress-related health problems (MacLeod and Meikle, 1994). Woods et al. (1997: 143) note that 'the number of teachers taking early retirement in England and Wales, for whatever reason, has risen by 68 per cent over the past decade, jumping by 50 per cent in 1988 – the year of the ERA – and climbing to a total of 17,798 in 1995'. The DfEE (1998a) statistics show that although there has been a fall in ill-health retirements in the 1989/90–1997/98 period (mainly because the rules regarding eligibility were changed following the compilation of the 1996–97 data) the 96–97 figures show an increase of 1,920 teachers, which represents a 53 per cent rise in the eight year period.

When the years 1989 and 1998 are compared, 3,800 more teachers took premature retirement in 1998. This shows an increase of 43 per cent. A growing number of headteachers, too, are retiring early, and vacant head-ships are increasingly not attracting as many applicants as they used to (Fisher, 1995). Teacher morale is reported to be at a low ebb (Smithers, 1989), particularly since the regulations on early retirement have changed, making leaving teaching for mid- and late career teachers difficult. Many are feeling 'locked in' and 'trapped in teaching' (Woods et al., 1997). There is a steady stream of articles in the educational press giving personal accounts of the experience of stress and burnout. There is also an increasing number of media accounts of teachers winning financial compensation through the law courts, from their employers, for illness and unemployment caused by stress-related illness induced by stressful work conditions including 'bullying' at work (see for example *Times Educational Supplement*, 14/1/2000 and O'Leary, 2000). The professional, career, emotional and identity cost to the individual and the educational and economic cost to the country is of a very high order and apparently worsening.

There is an 'explosion of insecurity' (Woods et al., 1997) in teaching, manifest in the numbers of redundancies and redeployments. The increased casualisation of teaching (Lawn, 1995), with temporary and short-term contracts, increases insecurity. The current crisis in the recruitment and retention of teachers indicates that teaching is arguably an increasingly unattractive profession for many. Some of the consequences of teacher illness and shortages are an increase in class sizes and in the numbers of supply teachers and teaching auxiliaries being employed. Menter et al. (1999) argue that the vacancy rates have created a culture of heavy reliance on supply teachers. Her Majesty's Inspectorate found that while the majority of sessions taught by supply teachers were satisfactory, there were long-term problems in planning, record keeping, and maintenance of equipment and the school environment. All of these factors impact negatively on pupil achievement.

The social context of teacher stress

Teacher stress has accompanied restructuring. In the context of the educa-tion system in England and Wales, restructuring has been under way since the late 1970s but has gained massive impetus through the ERA 1988 (Woods et al., 1997). Restructuring is a response to perceived educational inadequacies for the modern world. As teachers have been blamed for many of the problems in education it seems clear that restructuring has had major implications for teachers' work and their workplace (Dale, 1989). Policy prescriptions since the 1970s have consistently had teachers as their focus for change. Recent policies have redefined and reworked teachers and teaching (Seddon, 1991), and the new roles and responsibilities teachers are having to take up go well beyond classroom teaching (Webb and

Vulliamy, 1996). The reforms seem, to some, to be geared to producing efficient classroom technicians capable of 'delivering' the pre-packaged curriculum and tests (Apple, 1986).

Teachers' work cultures are also set to change. Advocates of restructuring aim to 'reculture' schools as workplaces through the introduction of new ways of managing teachers and the installation of work cultures likely to lead to successful implementation of the reforms (D. Hargreaves and Hopkins, 1991). While some see the changes as offering new challenges and opportunities leading to enhanced professionalism and the improvement of schooling (D. Hargreaves, 1994), others view them as promising to deskill, disempower and stress teachers (Menter et al., 1997).

The social context of the escalation of stress is the 'globalization of capital and communications, the rapid growth of information and technological developments, changed modes of economic production, economic crisis and increasing moral and scientific uncertainty' (Woods et al., 1997: 1). These global changes have transformed the nature of trust relationships in post-traditional societies (Giddens, 1991). Grace (1991) reminds us that the issues surrounding restructuring and the statistics indicating teacher stress, supply, retention and morale problems can only be understood in the socio-historical context of relations between the state and education. He argues that in over a century of struggle teaching is an occupation which, after being held in contempt at the beginning of the twentieth century, has, 'after periods of condescension, confrontation and distrust, moved towards a more co-operative phase of teacher–state relations' (ibid.: 4). By the mid-1970s teachers had come to be regarded by state agencies as trusted professionals who could be 'given extensive autonomy to define appropriate curriculum contents and appropriate methods of teaching and learning' (ibid.). The teachers knew their professional responsibilities and 'procedures of formal specification' (ibid.: 5) were not needed. However, Grace argues that these decades of struggle and advance towards being a professional occupation have been eliminated by the recent ideological attack from state agencies; and that, following more than two decades of restructuring in education, relations between teachers and the state now lie 'shattered'. In place of trust there is now widespread distrust of teachers (Helsby, 1999) evident in the loss of their relative autonomy (previously the source of professional pride) and the replacement of a 'culture of consultation' by one of 'imposition' (Grace, 1991: 11). Rather than having the autonomy enjoyed by other professions, teachers' work is tightly regulated, where they have an 'explicit contractual obligation' (ibid.: 7). The increased incidence of stress in the profession and the 'number of courses, conferences and publications now devoted to the study of teacher stress is one of the most obvious indicators of the crisis in teacher–state relations' (ibid.: 8).

Understanding the social context is important in stress studies because a great deal of research on stress has adopted 'the orthodox categorisation of the person as a psychological entity distinct from the social milieu, though influenced by it' (Handy, 1990: 5). Despite much psychological work in the area of teacher stress, we lack detailed testimony from teachers on how they experience and feel about work and how it has changed, and exactly how their work is now stress producing. This is one area we explore in the book, for existing teacher development studies suggest that how teachers feel about their work has a direct impact on their effectiveness, professional development and continuance in teaching (Nias, 1989; Jeffrey and Woods, 1996; Hargreaves, 1994 and 1998a). We know very little about teachers' experiences of stress, the coping strategies they use in dealing with it, and especially their processes of self-renewal following periods of stress-related illness. It also seems important to us to complement the existing body of stress research with a perspective which embraces the 'social' aspects of stress and stress-related illness (Fineman, 1995), while also 'addressing' the 'relationship between the (current) social environment and individual subjective experience' (Handy, 1995: 8).

The term 'stress' lacks a precise definition and is, therefore, a contested concept. By some definitions the whole of the teaching profession could be considered to be experiencing stress, and, indeed, an element of stress is probably inevitable and possibly educationally productive. Most professionals, it could be argued, work under pressure. By other definitions, only a small minority is seen to be affected, and this is often viewed as being due to the impact of personal and situational factors on the individual. There is a tendency here to individualise the problem and pathologise teachers. Rarely is stress considered as a social construct and as a response to structural forces. There is a need, therefore, to conceptualise stress within the interchange among macro, meso and micro factors. Woods (1996a: 1) argues that:

> Stress is a multi-dimensional and multi-levelled phenomenon, and personal (micro) situational (meso) and structural (macro) factors are involved in its production. It is an individually experienced phenomenon which is socially produced. There are certainly the personal elements of personality, commitment, career and role, and values involved. There are situational ones, too, of school organisation, teacher culture and teacher/pupil relationships. However, there are also wider factors such as the wholesale restructuring of schools and teaching which has been taking place in recent years.

We examine the interrelationships among the micro, meso and macro rather than treating them as discrete levels (Kelchtermans, 1995a). As Hargreaves (1998b: 422) argues, these levels are not 'tightly insulated from one another' and 'structure and agency are relationally connected'. We avoid an analysis which 'forces a false separation of self, structure and situation into different sites of experience' (ibid.). What is really important is to seek to understand how 'structures exert their effects and with what consequences and implications for the self, in different places and times' (ibid.). The recent restructuring and reculturing of education has provided an opportunity to study the 'interconnections between political frameworks and school and classroom structure and processes' (Woods, 1996b: 75). A focus on social processes in the school organization is important here (Leithwood et al., 1999). This point is recognised by Fineman (1995: 120) when he argues that:

> Though the personal experience of stress is decidedly individualistic, it is expressed through the cultural and political milieu of the organisation. By this, I mean firstly the differences in power, status, and control that socially structure an organisation, elements of which emanate from the broader society of which the organisation is a part.

We aim to describe the subjective experience of stressed primary school teachers and to explore the relationship between that experience and social context (Handy, 1990). Smylie (1995: 3) has argued that 'what is stressful depends . . . on how it is perceived'. Whilst we also acknowledge there are 'objective' sources of stress, one orientation of the book is to explore sources of stress in their work and personal lives as teachers perceive them. Self, role and career are major foci within this approach. Where there is a large investment of the self in role, as with many primary teachers especially (Nias, 1989), there is an increased risk. How are the recent changes affecting teachers' identity, commitment and concept of career?

Much previous research has been concerned with stress once it has occurred (Cockburn, 1996), focusing on individuals coping with stress, or looking at stress from a management perspective as a failing in individuals (Newton et al., 1995). We trace the sources of stress – partly to do with individuals, but mainly with the restructuring of schools and education, and changing work patterns in the institution, leading to changed roles and relationships in schools. We hope, therefore, that the findings of the research presented in this book can be used to inform government and institutional policy to help prevent occupational stress in teaching, and in other 'caring' professions, as well as helping teachers themselves who may be suffering from stress to cope and to recover.

Research methods

Our approach was qualitative, the principal method being semi-structured and open-ended, in-depth, life history interviewing. We sought a sample of primary teachers who had experienced stress in their work. In order to contact headteachers and teachers who were experiencing or had experienced stress, we collaborated with a local authority occupational health unit currently engaged in counselling employees (who were either self-referred, or referred by their GPs), of the local authority (largely teachers, social workers and fire service personnel) who are experiencing stress. All had been diagnosed by their GP or local authority doctor or independent psychiatrist as suffering from anxiety, depression or stress-related illness. The unit also had knowledge of those teachers who had returned to school or who had retired early or had otherwise left teaching for stress-related reasons. In terms of sampling, attendance at the unit for counselling, receiving medical treatment (or both) for stress-related illness and having a prolonged period off work, provided an operational definition of stress for our research. Teachers conforming to this definition were identified by the unit who circulated our letter to these teachers inviting them to take part in the research. Thus, we were reliant on an opportunity sample. Some of the respondents gave us further contacts, colleagues or friends who were receiving support from the unit, and this provided a small snowball sample.

The eventual core sample consisted of twenty teachers, thirteen women and seven men. These worked, or had worked in schools across a range of urban and rural locations. The gender proportions and ages represent those found in the teaching profession generally in that they were predominantly women and a large majority was forty years of age or above (Wragg et al., 1998). A range of positions was represented though the majority were subject co-ordinators, in mid- to late career, the significance of which we discuss in Chapter 4. There were three headteachers (two male, one female) and two newly qualified teachers (female). A range of adaptations was evident including teachers on sickness absence, those who had returned to work and some who had left teaching. Some characteristics of this group are shown in Table 0.1.

The teachers who participated were interviewed (by Geoff) in their homes. Each interview was normally of one-and-a-half to two hours duration, the length being determined by the interviewee. There were a minimum of two, and a maximum of five interviews with respondents over a two-year period. This added a longitudinal dimension to the research, enabling us to chart the 'stress career'.

Additionally, we conducted an organisational study of two primary schools involving observation and interview. This study was of two large primary schools located in different LEAs. One, in an urban area, and a self-defined 'low-stress' school, had recently received a highly favourable Ofsted report and had low teacher absence rates; low staff sickness rates; low staff turnover; and high teacher morale. The other, a self-defined 'high-stress school', was an inner city school under 'special measures' at the time of the research, having been defined by Ofsted as a 'failing' school. It was experiencing high levels of teacher stress, high staff turnover and high absence rates. While we draw on data collected at these schools throughout the book, details of the schools and the teachers are provided in the case studies reported in Chapters 1 and 5.

Table 0.1 Characteristics of the core sample of teachers

Teacher	Age	Position prior to stress illness	Current position	School location
Mary	53	Science & Assessment Co-ordinator KS1	Left teaching	Urban
Ben	39	Maths Co-ordinator KS2	Retirement on grounds of ill-health	Urban
Elizabeth	45	Art Co-ordinator KS2	Art Co-ordinator & Year Co-ordinator	Inner City
Susan	33	NQT KS1	Part-time class teacher	Rural
Merryl	35	Headteacher	Deputy headteacher	Rural
Henry	39	Deputy headteacher	Headteacher	Urban
Judith	46	Class teacher KS 2	Class teacher KS 2	Urban
Jackie	50	English Co-ordinator KS2	Extended sick leave	Inner City
Olivia	59	SEN Co-ordinator KS2	Part-time class teacher	Urban
Marion	51	Assessment Co-ordinator KS 1	Retirement on grounds of ill-health	Inner City
Anna	25	Class teacher KS1	Class teacher KS1	Urban
William	45	Science, IT & Games Co-ordinator KS2	Class teacher	Urban
Lorraine	36	Music Co-ordinator KS2	Class teacher	Urban
Joyce	45	Science Co-ordinator KS1	Left teaching	Rural
Thomas	46	Headteacher	Left teaching	Inner City
Jeremy	42	Humanities, Art & Technology Co-ordinator KS2	Extended sick leave	Inner City
Arthur	49	Headteacher	Headteacher	Rural
Barbara	52	Head of Infant Department	School liaison worker	Inner City
Pauline	60	Class Teacher	Retired	Rural
Michael	52	Science Co-ordinator KS2	Retired on grounds of ill-health	Urban

Geoff also carried out fieldwork with a teacher self-help group which had been set up by local authority employees, mostly teachers (also some private sector employees), who felt they had been 'bullied' at work, and in some cases, forced out of teaching. The group's aims were to give emotional and practical support to colleagues in the network; to publicise their situation and act as a pressure group devoted to raising these issues with employers and unions; and to bring about change in the workplace while seeking redress for their members. Geoff attended their monthly evening meetings and engaged in participant observation, enabling him to conduct the case study in parallel with work on the main project of interviewing and school studies.

All the teachers in the core sample were 'diminished' teachers, who were either 'leaving' the system or, during stress episodes, 'sinking' beneath it (Woods et al., 1997). It could be argued that teachers suffering from stress are in some way personally 'inadequate' or 'incompetent'. This seems unlikely, for the majority of the teachers participating in the research had considerable experience and records of being extremely able teachers.

It might be argued that such a sample, containing a majority suffering from stress-related illness, could be atypical of teachers generally. However, these teachers are dealing with the same educational changes affecting their work as all other teachers in the education system. Additionally, there are considerable numbers of teachers who report stress (Travers and Cooper, 1996) and those who are thinking of leaving (Dinham and Scott, 1996) or who have resigned (Dinham, 1992). The teachers in this sample, therefore, might be regarded as 'critical cases' in that they highlight issues common to all to some extent rather than peculiar to themselves (Hammersley and Atkinson, 1995).

All the names of teachers, headteachers, inspectors, schools and LEAs used in the book are pseudonyms.

The structure of the book

The first three chapters detail the onset of stress and its consequences, and the experiences of the teachers. The later chapters move on to identifying modes of recovery from stress with recommendations being made for its prevention. We begin in Chapter 1 by considering some of the sources of stress in primary teaching. Recent accounts of teacher emotions and cultures of teaching point to unsatisfactory social relationships between adults, for example, colleagues, headteachers, parents and inspectors, elicit hostile emotions from teachers. This chapter examines why this should be the case. Some argue that the intensification of work and government policies promoting managerialism in schools are the roots of the problem (Hargreaves, 1994; Woods et al., 1997). This chapter uses the teacher accounts to examine staff relationships in their schools. Forms of trust relationship are explored, suggesting that while intensification and managerialism are certainly involved in eroding positive staff relationships, they are partly products of the changing trust relations in society, and impacting negatively on teachers' physical and emotional well-being and on their collegial professional relations.

In Chapter 2, we focus on a specific example of a stressful workplace. Further consequences of a lack of trust in teachers are noted. The analysis is made through a case study of a self-defined high-stress school, an Ofsted defined 'failing' school, located in an inner city area of high social disadvantage with an ethnically diverse intake. This school was under 'special measures' and during this process experienced high staff turnover and absence rates. The case study examines factors associated with stress such as: teacher biography and values; staff relationships; teacher/pupil relationships; school/community relationships; headteacher leadership strategies; school organisation; working conditions; and school ethos. Recent education policy has sought school improvement through the public naming, blaming and shaming of 'failing' schools. These dominant discourses explain school failure largely in terms of incompetence in teaching and leadership. These views, however, do not penetrate the contradictions and complexities of social life in failing schools. This chapter seeks to explore the perspectives of those working in a 'failing school'. It examines the influencing factors that impact negatively on the majority of these teachers' physical and mental health resulting in them experiencing the negative emotions of shock, self-doubt, shame and inadequacy. For the majority of teachers, working in a 'failing' school was a negative experience, involving stress and breakdown, and termination of career. For a small minority, the experience resulted in professional enhancement.

In Chapter 3, we consider negative social relationships with a more detailed focus on the breakdown of trust within schools. In our research, we found that good staff relationships appeared to be an important source of job satisfaction in teaching. Equally, poor staff relationships were perceived by the teachers to be a major cause of stress, one aspect being the escalating phenomenon of 'bullying' among the staff. This appears generally to be on the increase (ATL, 1996). We consider reasons for the increase in 'bullying' in the workplace (teaching and other occupations) and explore the complexities and contradictions of 'bullying'. Some teachers in the study believed they had been forced out of teaching by 'bullying' management and felt marginalised, alienated and powerless. Some teachers viewed the controversial teacher 'competency' procedures as stressful, a form of 'bullying' in itself, and a method of dismissing teachers.

Following the experience of stress, some of our teachers left teaching prematurely; others continued in teaching, but with reduced roles. Chapter 4 explores these teachers' perspectives as they related to their careers and identities. Unpredictable and stress-induced breaks in teachers' careers are defined as 'fateful moments', involving a 'reassessment' and 'redefinition' of the teacher's self, commitment and career. This case study makes emerging patterns and experiences of teacher career in the conditions of 'late modernity' highly visible. We seek to show that unplanned disruption in careers can involve teachers in repeated re-inventions of the self, a stressful and convoluted process in itself.

Having considered sources of stress and some of their consequences for teacher identity and career we turn, in Chapter 5, to the strategies the teachers used to cope with stress in their work and lives. Stress posed a new threat to teacher identity. The coping strategies the teachers had developed throughout their careers proved inadequate to deal with this and new ones had to be developed. While we describe strategies in the other chapters (particularly in Chapter 4 on career adaptations), here we categorise them and focus on teachers generating and using personal resources, seeking alliances, and collective action. In some cases, coping strategies were successful and enabled the teachers to continue in their careers. In others, strategies only offered temporary respite and brought about a 'false recovery' (Carlyle, 1999). In these cases teachers subsequently left teaching.

In Chapter 6 we consider the characteristics of a 'low-stress school'. This case study reveals aspects of school culture, which prevent or ameliorate stress. We examine the school's organisational features and its teacher culture. The school had achieved success in its own and Ofsted's terms, staff turnover was low, morale was high. The pervasive nature of the discourse and practice of 'teamwork' in the school, which originated in and was maintained by trusting staff relationships, is described. Teacher culture was characterised by *openness, sharing, supporting, understanding* and *realism*. We make the case that this is a low-stress school owing to its particular informal organisation and culture. However, as a result of the Ofsted inspection, moves were being made to introduce more formal and standardised systems which, potentially, would threaten the high-trust–low-stress teacher culture and arguably raise teacher stress levels, which in turn would impact negatively on pupil achievement.

Chapter 7 sets out our recommendations for policy making at national, school and personal level. In particular, we consider the implications of organisational and cultural factors in the production and management of stress. Though there is support and advice in the book for those experiencing stress, the main emphasis is on how work organisations can best avoid creating stressful conditions for their workers. This, we believe, gets to the root of the problem – prevention is better than cure.

1 Teacher stress in the low-trust society

> In modern societies the antithesis of trust is a state of mind which could best be summed up as existential angst and dread.
> (Anthony Giddens, *The Consequences of Modernity*, 1990: 138)

Introduction

Commenting on the articles in a special edition of the *Cambridge Journal of Education* devoted to the topic of teacher emotions, Nias (1996: 300) observed:

> In this edition teachers' most extreme and negative feelings appear when they talk about their colleagues, the structures of schooling or the effect of changing educational policies upon them ... the most intensive, hostile and deeply disturbing emotions described in these articles came not from encounters with pupils or students, but with other adults, particularly colleagues, parents, school governors and inspectors. It is not clear why this shift should have occurred, nor whether it simply reflects a change in research priorities. It does, however, open up a fresh area of discussion and reflection for practitioners and academics alike.

Certainly many factors are at work in the production of stress in teaching. Teaching work in the primary school, for example, has changed radically during the last decade. Classroom teaching now constitutes only part of the teachers' work. Extra tasks involve work in planning and administration with colleagues, and work with parents and the community (Campbell and Neill, 1994; Webb and Vulliamy, 1996). The work of Woods (1995b), Jeffrey and Woods (1996), Woods et al. (1997), Menter et al. (1997), and Troman (1997) clearly note the negative effects of the intensification of work and managerialism on primary teachers and collegial relations in the primary school. In the context of secondary schooling, Ball (1988) uses labour process theory to explain that intensification involving the

separation of conception (managers) from execution (teachers) had fragmented staffs, creating an 'us and them' culture more characteristic of
industrial contexts. Not only was collegiality affected by this process. Gewirtz
(1996) and Reay (1996) found the teachers working in such conditions to
be experiencing high levels of stress. Evans (1992), in a rare study of primary
teacher morale and job satisfaction, found the situation-specific variables
of headteacher behaviour and staff relationships to be key factors influencing the teachers' satisfaction/dissatisfaction with teaching.

While all the above social processes are undoubtedly involved in teacher
stress and the breakdown in staff relationships, labour process theory may
have a limited explanatory power (Hargreaves, 1993) in revealing all that
is involved in the stress process and changing cultures of teaching. Our
research suggests that changing trust relations in society are reflected in
teachers' experiences in their work, with stressful consequences.

Trust and relationships

Trust between individuals and groups provides the basis for social order. It
is the mortar of solidarity and integration (Durkheim, 1956). Elster (1989)
argues that social order is characterised by the predictability of social life
and is maintained by the existence of habitual rules and social norms. A
normal and routine life would not be possible without 'an implicit and
unconsidered trust that everyday life does not carry major threats' (cited
in Misztal, 1996: p. 68). Hence, trust facilitates stability, co-operation and
cohesion.

Educational relationships cannot be established and maintained without
a strong bond of trust existing between teacher and pupils. Hargreaves
(1998a: 319) argues that teaching is an 'emotional practice' involving
trustful relationships with others. Trust is of prime importance in teaching
for its presence ensures that 'creative individuals are allowed greater
freedom and autonomy' (Alexander, 1989: 142). Trust is a precondition of
co-operation (Gambetta, 1988). High levels of trust are required amongst
participants (teachers, children and critical others) in 'critical events' for
the development of '*communitas* marked by a strong feeling of camaraderie,
a sense of common destiny, mutual support, the absence of stratification
by age, ability, social class, gender or race, the transcendence of status and
role as they apply in normal life, and great excitement and enthusiasm'
(Woods, 1995b: 93).

Nias et al. (1989) view trust as a prerequisite for effective and meaningful collaborative working relationships and argue that for trust to exist,
'people must find one another highly predictable and share substantially
the same aims' (ibid.: 81). Advocacy of collegiality in schooling is widespread. Little (1990) has 'advocated interdependence as the preferred and
most productive state of collegial relations among teachers' (in Hargreaves,
1998a: 324). Elias (1987) describes 'interdependence as the ideal state of

human relationships' (ibid.). Restructured organisations and cultures require collaborative, flexible and differentiated teachers to work in them (Lawn, 1995). They need to be able to work on their own, but also, increasingly, to work together. In the school improvement (Caldwell and Spinks, 1988; D. Hargreaves and Hopkins, 1991; D. Hargreaves, 1994) and teacher development (Fullan, 1991; Nias et al., 1989; Biott and Nias, 1992; Hargreaves, 1994) literature, there is a pronounced emphasis on collaboration through which teachers develop new skills by sharing professional knowledge. D. Hargreaves (1994) describes a 'new professionalism' in which teacher isolationism is broken down and a culture of collaboration arises. These views are supported by a number of official policy documents (DES, 1992; Ofsted, 1994) and in the Ofsted criteria for inspection (Ofsted, 1995). Caldwell and Spinks (1988) argue that devolved budgets and school self-management systems invest trust in schools to stimulate effectiveness and improvement initiatives. Trust in management to organise restructuring of the institution, to devise technically based solutions and implement radical reforms has been central to many of the recent changes (Walker and Barton, 1987; Inglis, 1989).

Trust is required for solid parent/teacher relationships which enhance children's learning (Bastiani, 1987). Since the 1950s there has been a marked change in the relations between the education state and parents. David (1992) argues that in the era of 'meritocracy' parents were held at arm's length from schools and seen to play no part in their child's education. There then followed a period of 'participation' in which they were viewed as co-educators. We are now experiencing the 'third wave' of 'parentocracy' (Brown, 1990). While there is not necessarily any reduction in levels of parent participation in schools, in the ideology of 'parentocracy' there is a groundswell of popular support for ideas concerning parents having a greater control over, and choice in, the education of their children. Parents as consumers are seeking the best buy in education. Parent power is in the ascendant (Dale, 1989). Such a change in relationship can weaken trust relationships between teachers and parents. Parents, as 'critical consumers', may force the 'pupil-teacher relationship into a transaction between a deliverer of a service and a customer' (Furedi, 1999: 37).

Trust and society

Giddens' extensive conceptual development of the nature of trust relations in high modernity draws 'recursive links between changes in society and individual dispositions' (Misztal, 1996). Trust, for example, cannot be understood without making reference to the allied concept of risk, variations of which are society related. Giddens (1990: 31) argues that:

> Where trust is involved, in Luhmann's view, alternatives are consciously borne in mind by the individual in deciding to follow a particular course

of action. Someone who buys a used car, instead of a new one, risks purchasing a dud. He or she places trust in the salesperson or the reputation of the firm to try to avoid this occurrence. Thus an individual who does not consider alternatives is in a situation of confidence, whereas someone who does recognise those alternatives and tries to counter the risks thus acknowledged, engages in trust.

While risk and danger certainly were features of life in pre-modern times:

> In simple societies, risk was associated with permanent danger; with threats of wild beasts, marauding raiders, famines and floods. Personal trust in family, friends and community helped people cope with these persistent risks. Risk in simple societies was something to be minimized or avoided. In modern, mass organizations and societies, risk and trust took on different qualities.
>
> (Hargreaves, 1994: 252)

Trust operates in environments of risk, in which varying levels of security (protection against dangers) can be achieved.

Giddens (1990: 34) defines trust as,

> confidence in the reliability of a person or system, regarding a given set of outcomes or events, where that confidence expresses a faith in the probity or love of another, or in the correctness of abstract principles.

For Giddens, trust in pre-modern societies was based on 'personal trust (trust in persons – facework commitment) secured by kinship, community, religion and traditions' (Misztal, 1996: 90). However, trust in high modernity (owing to the decline/fragmentation of traditional institutions and the increased division of labour and specialisation which means we must be lay persons in most matters) is based also on the abstract systems (faceless commitments) of *symbolic tokens* (media of interchange, such as money) and *expert systems* – that is 'systems of technical and professional knowledge where trust is based in a body of knowledge' (ibid.). However, Giddens argues that, in a period of high modernity where social relations have become *disembedded* from local contexts and 'recombined across time-space distances' (Giddens, 1990: 53), there is a 'renewed *re-embedding* and growing importance of personalised trust, based on deliberately cultivated face-to-face relationships' because they are more psychologically rewarding than trust in abstract systems (ibid.: 88).

Giddens also uses the concepts *basic* or *elementary* trust, often using them interchangeably. *Basic* trust is connected with the genesis of our *ontological security* – that is our confidence in the continuity of personal identity. *Elementary* trust is connected with the 'predictability of daily encounters'

(Misztal, 1996: 91). Without the development of *basic trust* (initially with parents, family, friends) people may experience 'existential anxiety, and lack of confidence in the continuity of their self-identity and the constancy of their environment' (ibid.).

With the breakdown of kinship, community, religion and tradition trust needs to be *negotiated*:

> Trust in persons is not focused by personalised connections within the local community and kinship networks. Trust on a personal level becomes a project, to be 'worked at' by the parties involved, and demands the *opening out of the individual to the other*. Where it cannot be controlled by fixed normative codes, trust has to be won, and the means of doing this are demonstrable warmth and openness.
>
> (Giddens, 1990: 121)

However, Giddens argues that in the 'high-risk society' (Beck, 1992) the consequences of the antithesis of trust are anxiety and dread. These are the 'debilitating effects of modern institutions on self-experience and the emotions' and are brought about through the absence or fracturing of trust (Giddens, 1990: 100).

The high-risk, low-trust society

We live in a *risk culture* (Giddens, 1990, 1991). Consequently there is a crisis of trust in society involving the breakdown of trusting relationships and the growth of distrust, not only within intimate and personal relationships, but also towards institutions (Castells, 1997). In globalisation, the social and geographical mobility of modern societies 'tends to erode trust and credibility by undermining the bonds of solidarity' (Misztal, 1996: 96). The plurality of views and values leads to uncertainty and distrust of experts. Deep distrust of out groups makes discrimination such as racism an endemic feature of social life. Suspicion and surveillance is evident in the proliferation of electronic equipment which overtly and covertly monitors behaviour in public spaces. There is public distrust of the unethical operations of some *expert systems*, for example transnational corporations. Fraud and bank collapse have fuelled the growth of regulatory bodies who monitor and attempt to control *expert systems*. For instance, the practice of auditing is so pervasive that most institutions (financial or not) are now subject to economic scrutiny and control of organisational procedures – this practice is so deeply embedded in the culture that the UK has been referred to as the 'audit society' (Power, 1994). There is currently a collapse of confidence in institutions in the Further Education sector in the UK as a number are being investigated for managerial impropriety and financial mismanagement. Distrust is evident in the low-trust management styles in Western societies (particularly UK and USA). The presence of conflict and a lack of mutual loyalty and responsibility between workers and bosses are features of low-trust workplaces (Kramer and Tyler, 1996).

Distrust of professionals is widespread. Misztal (1996: 201) explains that:

> Many surveys have found open distrust of political parties, a clear trend of declining public confidence in the democratic process and the growing alienation among many Westerners towards the bureaucratized political system.

In the medical sphere, doctors are increasingly the targets of litigation in widely publicised cases of negligence involving the injury and death of patients. In education, reforms were introduced in the context of a public 'discourse of derision' and were based on a profound distrust of teachers (Ball, 1994; Helsby, 1999). The moral panic concerning falling educational standards has continued to encourage the public's distrust of teachers. The introduction in 1992 of the regulatory body of Ofsted inspections and league tables, whose aim is to restore confidence and trust in education and minimise the risk of failure by the regulation and control of teachers' work and processes of schooling, have themselves become the object of distrust by some teachers, educationists and education researchers (see, for example, Ofstin, 1997).

The nature of trust relations in schooling

Research in industrial settings has shown the centrality of trust dynamics in workplace cultures. For example, Fox (1974) has used Gouldner's *Patterns of Industrial Bureaucracy* and *Wildcat Strike* (1955 and 1965) to show how high-trust relations in the workplace are positively linked with high job satisfaction and productivity in spite of low wage-rates. Conversely, low-trust relations (including close and punitive supervision and the imposition of strict bureaucratic rules) violate the psychological contract between workers and managers, despite increased wages. This change in trust relations resulted in reduced job satisfaction and industrial conflict. Thus, in some contexts, the social and psychic rewards of work appear more important than the material ones.

'Vulnerability' and 'giving trust' and 'wanting to be trusted' were key themes running through our respondents' testimonies (see also Kelchtermans, 1996). The focus here, therefore, is on categories of trust–distrust and their impact on the physical and emotional well-being of individual teachers and their personal and collegial relations. The categories are:

TRUST	DISTRUST
Intimacy	*Alienation*
Togetherness	*Antagonism*
Supportive	*Undermining*

Mutuality	*Isolation*
Security	*Insecurity*
Acceptance	*Suspicion*

Intimacy – alienation

Some of the teachers experienced a breakdown in close and intimate personal relationships leading to alienation at home and at work. Traditional family structure and lifestyle are changing rapidly in high modernity (Castells, 1997). The patriarchal nuclear family is no longer the norm owing to the breakdown of trusting relationships and new forms of intimate relationships arising (Giddens, 1990, 1991). The majority of the teachers appeared to enjoy trusting and supportive intimate relationships that enabled them to cope with their illness. But, for some, chronic strains (Pearlin, 1989) in the life-world (Kelchtermans, 1995b) involved difficulties in or a break-up of a personal relationship. Two of the teachers had severely disabled children to raise. This caused tension in their relationships with their partners and contributed to an already stressful situation at work. One divorce resulted from this situation. In some cases, stressful domestic events were paralleled with stressful circumstances at work. Mary thought she was 'untypical' of other stressed teachers in that she viewed her domestic situation as the prime factor in her stress illness. She was untypical in the sense that her intimate relationship had ended in extremely violent and acrimonious circumstances. However, her case shows graphically the negative impact of an interrelation of influencing factors arising in both professional and personal lives. Stress from school would spill over into the home and exacerbate the stress being experienced by her partner. Stress from home would spill into her workplace. This emotional interplay is evident in the following:

> MARY: The first three years we were together things were all right. But then I knew that he was very fond of drinking and it became increasingly obvious to me that he was an alcoholic. And this is why I said I might not be typical for your research because I'd been under tremendous pressure at school with this Ofsted inspection coming up. And also tremendous pressure at home because of him being an alcoholic. What used to frequently happen was that he would go up the pub of an evening. He'd come back stupidly drunk and he would harangue me about my shortcomings for as long as he could. And he said I'd got lots so he would do a different selection every single night.
>
> GEOFF: What sort of things were they?
>
> MARY: He'd probably say that I was a rotten teacher, that I was a rotten cook, that I was Irish, and I thought originally that my appeal to him was the fact that I was Irish. He said he loved Ireland. Oh,

all sorts of different things, you know. Anything that came into his head he would harangue me about and –

GEOFF: Was he a teacher as well?

MARY: No he wasn't. I think this was part of the problem, he didn't realise the pressures that teachers had, that you had to work in the evening, although I did try to stay at school as late as I could and do as much as I could at work. He was a boat builder. Of course the recession affected that industry very badly and in fact it's only getting out of it now. And he's an excellent worker, people spoke very highly of his work, but there was less and less work around. So, of course, financially he was also becoming more and more dependent on me. And I had to take over the mortgage which was quite large because we'd bought a big house. And after he'd harangued me, which didn't do wonders for my self-esteem, he would play music very loudly underneath the room in which I slept where there was a chimneybreast. So of course the noise would come right up to the room. And he'd play it till two, three, four o'clock in the morning which was devastating when I had to get up and be bright-eyed and bushy-tailed at school at half past eight. My self-esteem has been shattered by him.

Following the type of experience described here and the resulting illness, loss of self-esteem and confidence, Mary's performance as an infant teacher plummeted, and following a long period off work she eventually returned to face competency proceedings involving the breakdown of trust at school (see Acceptance – Suspicion below).

Togetherness – antagonism

All respondents were quite clear about the importance of close staff relationships – 'togetherness'. Human exchanges in genuinely collaborative teacher cultures made work more pleasant and served to reduce stress. Pressures of intensification led to antagonistic relationships between teachers and pupils. Susan, an NQT who recently resigned her post in a stressful school owing to poor staff relationships and a breakdown in trust of the headteacher, reflects on her very different experiences and warmth of relationships in her teaching practice schools:

Without a shadow of a doubt I would say that the school that I've just left is populated by very grey, very knackered looking people. And I just don't understand why, it just seems like there's a culture of over-work and a culture of over-bureaucracy. Both my practice schools were terrific. They had a sense of togetherness. They had a sense of fun. They had a sense of humour that you could go and have a laugh with somebody about a problem. And they could support you and perhaps suggest some things and then ask you how they were going. But all in a very, very non-threatening, helpful way. I went to see one of them on the way back from University last week when I was trying to decide what to do. I thought I'll just drop in and see one of my practice schools. And I went in there and it was after the children had gone. And the first two members of staff I saw just ran out and gave me a big hug.

Elizabeth found the work of integrating children with EBD and catering for the full range of pupil achievement in a context of financial cuts and large classes very stressful. In these circumstances she was clearly finding it difficult to form warm and trusting relationships with many of the pupils. Talking of her class, she said:

We have a lot of SEN. We've only got a part time SEN coordinator. And not enough LSAs to go round really. So there's one class for example that I have – a year five class – which has six children in it with EBD needs and I don't have any help. So it's me, thirty ordinary children, six of whom have EBD problems and there's paint everywhere and I'm expected to run an interesting and creative practical class with children who can be really difficult to manage. Which means that a lot of children are neglected. Because I just cannot be everywhere at once. And it also limits the work you can do. So you really have to slow down and take things in easy steps. So then it's really difficult to challenge the brighter ones because you're spending so much time inputting for these other children to keep them on task and keep them cheerful and working along in a positive way. I just find it really really wearing to keep meaningful activities going as opposed to control. So that's a real problem.

Some of the teachers were locked into a stress cycle where exhaustion contributed to worsening teacher/pupil relationships which in turn induced further exhaustion and impacted on teacher efficacy:

SUSAN: I'm exhausted and being exhausted is actually affecting my performance in the classroom. Because I'd started to notice that certainly by the end of the week I was getting to a stage where I just was not functioning as I would be running low on fuel. Things were getting to me that wouldn't have got to me on a Monday. And I was noticing that at the end of the week I was just getting a little bit tetchier – children's behaviour that I would have dealt with in one way perhaps on a Monday or whatever – I was just getting so tired by a Friday that the kids would wind me up more.

A gradual wearing away is evident in Susan's account. While providing data on teacher sense of self-efficacy and stress this raises interesting questions concerning the pupils' reactions to their teacher's stressed behaviour. It is possible that the teacher's level of tolerance is lowered as exhaustion sets in. Equally, the pupils may read the signs (for example teacher body language, linguistic 'tetchiness') and 'suss out' (Beynon, 1984) that the teacher is not operating as effectively as usual, and try and maximise their own 'interests at hand' (Pollard, 1985) in escalating misbehaviour. An outcome of this process is the erosion of warm teacher/pupil relationships.

Some of the teachers had good reasons to distrust some of their pupils. Unlike Nias' (1996) teachers, those here reported many incidents in which the hostile behaviour of pupils had been the source of stress and impacted negatively on school collegiality. Only one respondent reported being physically assaulted by a pupil (year three boy) but others told of colleagues who had been threatened with violence, sometimes by quite young children. Judith, the teacher who had been physically attacked, said that she had started teaching as a mature entrant with an extremely disruptive group of children whom she described as the 'class from hell' (see also Lawrence and Steed, 1986).

Many writers have argued that teachers derive their job satisfaction from the psychic rewards of teaching (Lortie, 1975; Rosenholtz, 1989; Hargreaves, 1998a). Central amongst these is the development of close relationships and 'emotional understanding' (Hargreaves, 1998a). In the examples we have seen here there seems little space for this type of emotional work.

Supportive – undermining

All the teachers recognised the importance of trusting relationships and human and professional support from colleagues. They particularly valued a supportive and encouraging attitude from the headteacher. However, support for the teachers' professionality was sometimes not forthcoming. Indeed some headteachers undermined the teachers' sense of efficacy and professionalism. For example, even though the probationary year is known to be particularly stressful (Nias, 1989; Huberman, 1993; Cains and Brown, 1998), Anna actually found subsequent years in a less emotionally supportive teacher culture more difficult:

> I found it very, very hard. But looking back on it now my first year was my easiest year, I think. And I've found that it's got harder each year. Which is on the head to toe of what I thought it would be like. I thought the first year would be very hard. My first year I had a very good mentor who supported me, kind of helped me and supported me through it.

All the teachers stated that they could not work effectively without the support of their headteachers. However, this was often denied them. Susan, for example, requested support in dealing with an incident in her class and wanted her headteacher to discipline a pupil who was involved:

> And before I know it I'm having it turned round. She said, 'You must not lead other people to think ill of the children and you must be very careful what you say.' And I'm thinking, 'I came in here with a child that an LSA has seen do something to another child, and not only had she seen him do it once but seen him do it twice. And he's sitting out there and I'm expecting you to tear him off a strip and I'm the one who's being torn off a strip.' And I went out extremely confused and extremely unhappy. And basically resolving never ever to go in there with a problem again because as far as I'm concerned I have not been supported at all. In fact as far as I'm concerned every problem that I've gone in with the spotlight's been turned on me much as to say, 'Well, what are you doing wrong? What are you doing to cause this?'

Hargreaves (1998a: 324) argues that when a teacher asks a colleague for help 'they place their confidence and perceived competence on the line. Their professional persona and sense of self is put at risk' (see also Dadds, 1993). A consequence of the kind of interaction experienced by Susan is what Giddens (1990: 98) argues is:

> a suspension of trust in the other as a reliable, competent agent, and a flooding in of existential anxiety that takes the form of hurt, puzzlement and betrayal together with suspicion and hostility.

Elizabeth's headteacher did not support staff and evaded major problems in the school. She appeared more trusting of pupils than teachers but rather than implying unprofessionality in the teachers, as Susan's headteacher had done, she used the strategy of confrontation avoidance:

> I think any child who threatens a member of staff like that something's got to happen. It's not condoned but it's sort of glossed over. She's (headteacher) a great one for glossing over things and not tackling them. So children get too powerful in that situation. As I said before we've got a lot of children who are leading sort of fairly disordered lives and they need a velvet glove with an iron fist in it. But she's got the velvet glove and inside is more velvet and it's just not effective. She doesn't – there's lots of things wrong, like there's no presence around the school; she hides in the office.

This headteacher was later accused of incompetence by her staff and, following a vote of no confidence by staff and governors, resigned her post.

Jackie supported the National Curriculum and, like others in the study, felt let down by a headteacher who was not committed to its implementation. She was seeking to promote academic values which were opposed to the impression management, marketing strategies and anti-National Curriculum stance of the headteacher:

JACKIE: That was one of the things where I didn't agree with the head. I felt I was there to teach the subject and that all the other niceties were there to support the teaching of the subject.

GEOFF: What do you mean by 'other niceties'?

JACKIE: Having links with the community, having an anti-bullying policy *for the children*. It didn't actually function that well but it looked good on paper. We had all these pictures in the paper of the teachers and kids doing weird and wacky things. The skeleton of the curriculum was just not at all there. He didn't believe in the National Curriculum, he didn't think that it was necessary. I don't know what he did believe in. But he used to ridicule staff who were very serious about their jobs which made me wonder if he felt inadequate himself. I don't think people do that unless they've got some chip on their shoulder. He'd do it publicly. I just wonder whether he had enough of a background in academic subjects to realise what we were trying to do. And if he did realise what we were trying to do I don't know what he was playing at, because he did try to undermine teaching and disciplining the children.

Such headteachers were viewed by their staffs as incompetent and provoked negative emotions (Blase and Anderson, 1995). They did not value positive human relationships in or outside work. As Judith explained:

We were treated badly. It didn't matter that we had any lives.

These headteachers did not support by giving positive feedback on their staffs' work. Elizabeth felt affirmed by a glowing report from Ofsted on her work. She had never previously received praise from her headteacher who would 'not know what a good job I was doing, but even if she did wouldn't say anything nice'.

Mutuality – isolation

In some of the study schools there was genuine mutuality in the sense that the teachers were dependent on each other in dealing with difficulties in their work and lives. In others, individuals were becoming socially isolated from their colleagues. In some schools, collaboration had become compulsory in order to aid restructuring. But in practice this form of collaboration sometimes took the form of 'contrived collegiality' (Hargreaves, 1994). Some of the schools in the stress research had adopted what on the face of it were collegial arrangements for planning and decision-making. However, the trust invested in the teachers was, in some cases, heavily bounded. For example, in Susan's school collegial decision-making was expected by management but the issues involved were considered rather trivial:

> SUSAN: I think it's bureaucracy gone mad. Personally, having worked in a completely different environment I do not understand why I have to be in a meeting which discusses the kitchen staff – discusses things that I as an ordinary class teacher do not need to know about. For goodness sake there's a senior management in the school, senior management in schools are the people who need to know about these things. I am a normal class teacher. I do not need to know about these things. I need to be sent a memo about them, but I don't need to sit there when I could be doing other things.
>
> GEOFF: Why have you had to discuss kitchen staff?
>
> SUSAN: Well it just comes up. And I'm sitting there thinking I'm going to explode in a minute. I'm going to tell them. But we all sit there. And those kind of things possibly come up in morning meetings or whatever. But there seems to be a need to involve every member of staff in every decision and I'm going through policies and they'll be talking about whether there should be an 'and' there or an 'and also'. And whether that full stop should be there or whether that comma should be there. And I did actually say at one point, 'It really doesn't make any difference. It really does not make any difference.' But there seems to be an over obsession with involving everybody with everything – well to the point where every single member of staff has to look over every single policy and change the words about. Not change the policies but just change the words about, very slightly; tinkering. This is just a ridiculous waste of people's time when people are very, very busy.

Other studies (Evans, 1992; Brown and Ralph, 1998) have shown that a source of stress in teaching was that teachers were not included in key decision-making in their schools. Attendance at meetings involving the type of experience described above was one source of Susan's stress. She argued that management organised what to her were meaningless meetings in order to satisfy Ofsted that collective decision-making took place in the school. Thus, they were of symbolic rather than practical value.

Financial cuts which involved the removal of non-contact time for staff had brought about emotional turbulence in staff relationships and a breakdown in trust between teachers and managers in the school where Henry was deputy headteacher:

There were staff who on the one hand would be coming emotional in tears, but also would stand there and scream and shout: 'I need my non-contact time'. 'This isn't right.' I mean shouting. And it would be at me, as if it's my fault because I'm the message bearer. But at quarter to nine in the morning if that happens on enough occasions you're beginning to twitch every time you're writing something up on the noticeboard. You're waiting for it to happen. And for all the, 'it's not my fault; there's nothing I can do about it; this is unreasonable', I find being shouted at by staff stressful. I know it's part of my role as deputy to handle staff who are feeling stressed and whatever. And at times I'm tempted to turn round and say, 'Oh shut up!' But you can't do that.

Ben was stressed by duties, pastoral work and planning for teaching:

What really got me more than anything else is not being able to take a break during the day. The morning break was about fifteen minutes. By the time you'd got the kids out and shushed the stragglers out the corridor, you were lucky if you had time to drink your coffee before it was time to start again. And at lunchtime – the so-called hour's break – you were usually getting things ready for the afternoon or looking after a child. You got about ten minutes to gobble down your sandwiches.

With the intensification of work, teachers have less time in 'back regions' (Goffman, 1959), such as breaks in staffrooms in which to socialise with colleagues. There is, therefore, less informal personal interaction of the kind which induces personal trust. Social relationships in primary schooling, as a result, are becoming more formalised.

Security – insecurity

Security refers to feelings of confidence in the face of risks or danger. Some of the teachers experienced threats to their physical and psychological security. Teaching was once seen as a secure occupation – a job for life (Lortie, 1975; Woods et al., 1997). However, this is increasingly not the case as short-term contracts and part-time working arrangements proliferate (Lawn, 1995).

Some headteachers, in their business manager roles, and faced with new forms of governance and unfamiliar aspects of management, such as personnel matters in the context of financial cuts, have brought about a separation of managers and teachers in some schools. Judith, for example, was made redundant in the following circumstances:

In 1990 they had to lose somebody so I actually received a redundancy notice in May which wasn't done correctly either, because the governors had never done it before and they didn't know how to do it. So there was a lot of hassle about it and the unions became involved and it was also very difficult and caused a lot of ill-feeling and mistrust. Everybody was kind of closing in and keeping things to themselves because everybody was anxious thinking, 'Is it going to be LSAs or is it going to be me? Is someone else going to take early retirement?'

The atmosphere of distrust undermines collegiality. The situation above sets teacher against teacher as they attempt to calculate their utility value to the school (Menter et al., 1997). Heterogeneity is increasingly evident in the workforce of primary schools with a core of permanent teachers and a periphery of part-time and temporary contract teachers (Lawn, 1995). The impact of this arrangement is divisive rather than integrative.

Olivia's headteacher had formerly been a friendly colleague but was now responding to pressures for her to be more managerial in her approach and was creating a climate of criticism:

The original teamwork had long since gone by now. Because originally the kids would try and get at us saying, 'Oh well, you two are friends, you obviously support one another'. It was very obvious to the kids that that was the relationship we had. It was only friendship within the school situation. We didn't meet outside school. But it was obvious to everybody that we got on well. But that all changed. Now she's undermining my status, she's setting me an impossible workload, she's not acknowledging any value in the work that I do, which didn't worry me really because I worked to my own standards, creating a critical atmosphere. I hated any meeting with her because I knew it was going to be a catalogue of what I hadn't done. And yet they were supposed to be supervision meetings. And senior management meetings. How can you have a senior management meeting with just two staff? I don't know. Suddenly changing – goal posts changing like nobody's business. Suddenly changing her position which created insecurity. You suddenly realised that what you thought was the unwritten rule of procedure she would suddenly change and we were doing something else.

Here Judith and Olivia have a lack of 'elementary trust in the possible intentions of others' (Giddens, 1990: 82). For an individual to feel psychologically secure they need continuity and reliability in personal relationships (Giddens, 1990, 1991).

Acceptance – suspicion

The professionalism of the teachers was not accepted, assumed or taken on faith by some groups. Thus, the teachers were under suspicion and under surveillance on a 'partial or unconfirmed belief that something is wrong or someone is guilty' (*Concise Oxford Dictionary*, 1976).

The 'official' distrust of teachers embodied in the new accountability systems was a source of stress in Marion's work and life. Before experiencing stress and later burnout, Marion seems to have had a moral commitment to her pupils, parents and colleagues. With the impending Ofsted inspection, legal accountability took over and the opposing values of Ofsted looked certain to provide a 'head-on collision' with Marion's values. Accountability took on a life of its own, 'just doing things for someone else to read'. Accountability was the source of a great deal of compulsion in her work – 'I had to do it'. In the early stages of illness (at home) she tried to catch up with 'accountability' paperwork for the inspection. She also wrote lists of household tasks she had completed in order to be accountable to her husband. Now retirement is seen by her as an escape from legal to self-accountability. 'There is still a great need to justify my existence. But it's only to me. No one is expecting me to say what I've been doing and account for my day, minute by minute.'

Mistrust of teachers' professionality meant they experienced multiple accountability pressures:

> Then it came to the inspection. The amount of paperwork that one has to do then is just crazy. And I'd said that I needed more time to do this. And again it just wasn't possible really to fund it. And I could feel it all happening again. I could see all the signs – the irritability, the crying.

A number of the teachers had become ill prior to the inspection and were absent from school when it took place. Mary explained that:

> In the week just before I had the breakdown, the Ofsted inspection was looming, also appraisals, SATs and parents' evenings. It was unfortunate, but all those came at one point. So it was just overwhelming, I just couldn't cope with it and woke up in the middle of the night sobbing uncontrollably.

The teachers felt they needed to produce much documentary evidence as proof of their professionalism. Ben and his school received an excellent Ofsted report but found the build-up to it contributed to intensification and was extremely stressful:

It was just hell really. And I felt that all the staff were very stressed, particularly at the time we had the inspection in January. The amount of preparation for that – and we were a school who were well prepared for it I think. But it was still planning. Yes you have to plan. You have to plan things carefully. But you've got daily plans, weekly plans, medium term plans, long term plans. There were plans coming out of our ears. Files and files to give to the inspectors with all these plans in. And I know damned well other schools that I've taught in weren't anywhere near as geared up for it. And we came out of it very well. But the amount of work involved in preparing for the visit was enormous. So we did all this extra work on top of the normal work which was taking up our evenings and our weekends.

Good parent/teacher relationships require high levels of trust. However, in the stress research the parents were sometimes distrustful of the teachers. For instance, Merryl, as headteacher of a small school, experienced stressful conditions involving changed powers of governors and parent power (Merryl fearing the withdrawal of pupils with the inevitable impact on the budget of a small school):

The governing body were very much people who would come and talk, would say things had to be done, and then go away and leave me to do it. There was one governor who was supportive and helped me draft policies but the others were not supportive. And there was one particular governor – I've never ever met a woman like her before and I never want to again. I understand she was actually invited on to the governing body before I started because she was regarded to be safer in the system than outside criticising. It was thought that if she had some responsibility for the school she couldn't do as much damage.

One day Merryl became involved when the son of this governor had a 'tantrum' in a colleague's class and ran out of school:

Then I had to go and find him and try and calm him down, try and sort him out and keep coming back to looking after my own class all the time knowing that I would have to confront the mother at the end of the day. She was not very supportive of the school at all. I think it was because perhaps she felt it was criticism of her as a parent. She basically didn't want to know. It was the school's problem. The school had to sort it out.

Teachers are now more directly accountable to parents. Mary (mentioned earlier), a teacher of twenty-five years experience, returned to school after a term's absence and was told by her headteacher that:

There were letters from parents. I don't know whether they were complaints, but they felt that this was why they wanted to see me. And my union official and I were only given a very, very brief glance at these letters and they were from a group of middle class parents. Now, I didn't think I was under-functioning but I obviously must have been. My doctor said I probably was as I was suffering from angina symptoms – severe chest pains. But they were a group of middle class parents who were very friendly in church and the union rep thought that they'd probably rubbed each other up. Now they said that I was being kind and considerate with the children and all this sort of thing. But I hadn't stretched them sufficiently intellectually.

Mary is now facing the recently introduced 'competency procedures' which can lead onto the 'fast-track dismissal system' (Wragg et al., 1998). This involved having her planning supervised and teaching monitored in class-room observations by deputy headteacher, headteacher and LEA inspector in individual visits phased over a term.

Henry had experienced the joint impact of pupils' manipulation and parent power and felt that teachers were increasingly distrusted by pupils:

I have seen a difference in parents' interactions with staff in recent years. Parents are much more prepared to be critical. Much more prepared to come in if they feel that something unfair or unjust or inappropriate has happened. Often based on either misinformation or partial information. There was a time, and I'm aware that I was on the tail end of it, but previously if you were in trouble at school and the chances were if you went home and told your parents you'd be in trouble at home as well. That's not the case now. There are many more, if you're in trouble at school, 'Oh that's not fair!'. I've had several instances recently where children have been dealt with, I'm quite convinced fairly, within the school, but for quite severe issues. And I've heard the children at home at the end of the day screaming and ranting and raving at their parents and because of that their parents are coming back to me and saying, 'This isn't right, I want this changed. I want something done about it'. Parents are to an extent being black-mailed and pressured by children. Children aren't allowed to go home crying and upset because they're being told off in school. You know, all children think it's not fair because they came off worse. And I'm finding that much more common.

Following recent exposures of abuse in schools and children's homes there is a breakdown in trust in public institutions which are intended to perform a caring role with children (Castells, 1998). We were given some accounts of teachers who had been accused of physical or sexual abuse of children at school. While the accusations were later found to lack any substance and the teachers were cleared, the breach of trust in them as teachers and people had resulted in the termination of their career in teaching and a breakdown in physical and mental health. It is this aspect of teaching work and the risks involved that Johnston et al. (1999) and Thornton (1999) argue is deterring young men from entering primary teaching.

Conclusion

Giddens' (1991: 2) theoretical framework is useful for viewing the nature of trust negotiations in schools. However, it requires empirical underpinning and development. The theory, by conflating agency with structure, takes us away from dualist conceptions of society to enable accounts of the social world in which:

> The self is not a passive entity, determined by external influences; in forging their self identities, no matter how local their specific contexts of action, individuals contribute to and directly promote social influences that are global in their consequences and implications.

Not all the teachers in this study worked at schools in which distrust had become physically and emotionally damaging. Some enjoyed positive personal and collegial relationships in their work. However, the majority did not. There were also examples of teachers' resistances to oppressive work regimes leading to changes being made to the 'system' at school level which brought about improvements in the psychic lives of the teachers. All this is consistent with Giddens (1990, 1991). For viewing events not as deterministic outcomes of social forces but as a dialectical process between agency and structure 'change is an ever present possibility' (Shilling, 1992: 80). However, in late modernity there is no certainty or inevitability; closure is difficult.

Giddens (1990: 6) recognises that modern institutions 'hold out the possibility of emancipation but at the same time create mechanisms of suppression, rather than actualisation, of self'. However, the evidence from this study can be used to question the theory. For instance, it does not fully consider the contexts within which the trust negotiations between individuals and groups are taking place or the extent of existential anxiety and dread that is generated in these interactions. Giddens does not fully engage with issues of the 'degrees of freedom that differentially placed agents have within a concrete structural situation' (Willmott, 1999a: 9). Actors in this case study, although not always devoid of agency, were heavily constrained, in situations where the educational system 'contextually limits what can be done, by whom and where' (ibid.). Manifestations of power and authority that are strongly evident in the empirical account do not seem adequately explained by the theoretical account (see also Willmott, 1999b).

In terms of education policy, it is always possible that problems experienced at the implementation stage may react back on the context of influence, thus leading to policy reformulation. Recent examples of this process would be the national boycott on SATs, and knowledge of teacher work overload leading to policy review and amendment (Dearing, 1994). The micro-politics of policy can 'force policy adjustments at the centre' (Fitz et al., 1994: 60). However, the current study does not offer unbridled optimism concerning the 'recursive nature' of the policy cycle (ibid.). Rather than policy makers listening to teachers' views on their changed work, there now seems to be a consensus and political will amongst the two major political parties that school improvement is to be sought by further tightening the control of teachers' work.

Apart from the personal (emotional and physical) and economic costs to the system resulting from the breakdown of personal relationships described in this chapter, there is a further consequence. The participants in primary education are now engaged in the mutual surveillance and documenting of each other's activities as the social relations of the primary school become more formalised. Management monitor and appraise teachers and keep files on teachers' behaviour and performance. Attempts to gain security are sought in legal and quasi-legal ways. Some of the teachers of this research keep dossiers which record incidents, and at all meetings with management they are accompanied by a 'professional friend' to act as a witness and note-taker. Evidence compiled in this way can later be produced at an industrial tribunal. Security seeking can also be seen in the proliferation of contracts. Management tightly specify the tasks to be accomplished in employment contracts and job descriptions. Whether this work is being produced or not, and its quality, are then established by monitoring, appraisal, teacher competency schemes and inspection by Ofsted. Parent/teacher relations are formalised through the introduction of home/school contracts. The unions and teachers involved in this study seek regulations and legislation on health and safety in the workplace which addresses such issues as occupational stress and workplace harassment.

Thus, there is a shift evident here from what Weber (1947) termed 'status' contracts to 'purposive' contracts. Fox (1974: 153) describes 'status' contracts as 'voluntary agreements for the creation of a continuing relationship' such as are found in comradeship. Alternatively, a 'purposive' contract is made to:

> complete a specific transaction or to further a discrete objective. Only a tenuous and temporary association is created. The purposive contract is infused with the spirit of restraint and delimitation: open-ended obligations are alien to its nature; arms-length negotiation is the keynote.

This is the shape that reform is taking in the UK. The recently proposed measures in the *Green Paper* (DfEE, 1998) intended to increase teacher motivation, job satisfaction and morale and make teaching a more attrac-tive and 'modern' profession by the introduction of firmer appraisal and performance related pay are, if the analysis in this chapter is correct, likely to bring about the opposite effects. The proposals, if introduced into schools, seem set to increase divisiveness and lead to further erosion of trust between the participants in primary schooling.

2 Failing schools, failing education

Introduction

Under the School Inspection Act 1996 (see Ofsted, 1999), consolidating earlier Acts, inspectors are advised that 'if the judgement is made that a school is failing or is likely to fail to provide acceptable standards of education, and Her Majesty's Chief Inspector agrees, the school is made subject to special measures' (Ofsted, 1999: 1). The special measures procedures require the production of an action plan addressing the key issues in the inspectors' report, which is sent to Ofsted and to the DfEE. The school then receives a visit from a member of Ofsted's School Improvement Division about once a term, until it is deemed that the school is providing an acceptable standard of education. An important part of the procedure is to identify publicly such 'failing schools' in the belief that improvement is all the more likely to come through 'naming, blaming and shaming'.

Schools that have been through this process do improve in some ways – unsurprisingly given the extra resources that are made available or a key change in management that occurs (Scanlon, 1999). The question is – at what cost? Do the ends justify the means? And how right is it anyway to explain school 'failure' in terms of incompetence and leadership? In a recent survey of schools that have been placed under special measures, a majority of which were primary, compared with a similar number that have not, Scanlon reports resentment, tension and divisions among the staffs as some were seen to 'pass' and others 'fail', and worsening relationships between headteachers and their staffs. There was a marked deterioration in staff morale among teachers in both groups. Some schools had problems of recruitment and retention. Most of Scanlon's teachers, while acknowledging improvements, felt that: 'There were better and more cost effective ways of achieving the same ends. . . . It had also created new problems or aggravated existing ones' (ibid.: 82).

We draw on a study of one such school to highlight some of the issues. We argue that the costs of the exercise outweigh the benefits. 'Improvement' might occur at a technicist level, as indicated by measurable tests, but at a cost to other aspects of what teachers regarded as a full education, such as creativity, education of the whole child, caring and sharing, multicultural education. Central to these concerns is the 'professional' teacher, equipped with wide-ranging skills and knowledge (including that of the local area and cultures within it), possessing a certain autonomy, able to exercise judgement, and peer-oriented in respect of support and development. Holding their professionalism together is a positive use of the emotions (Hargreaves, 1999a). They are vocational teachers, passionate about their work (Nias, 1989), who invest a great deal of their energies in motivating and inspiring their students, making emotional connections with them (Woods and Jeffrey, 1996), developing atmospheres and tones, creating new situations, new ways of doing things, continually renewing themselves.

This concept of professionalism has been largely overthrown by recent educational policy with its emphasis on economic rationality. For most of the teachers in our case study school, their experience of shock, self-doubt and feelings of shame and inadequacy undermined their confidence and devalued their expertise. It transformed positive into negative emotions. In consequence, they felt deprofessionalised (see also Jeffrey and Woods, 1998) and demoralised (Nias, 1991). The current headteacher, when reflecting on the personal cost to him and his staff of getting out of special measures, said, 'There must be a better way'.

The case study school and research methods

Gladstone Street Primary School is situated close to the centre of a southern English city and is located in a district of dense pre-war terraced brick housing. The area shows evidence of urban decay and deprivation. Ofsted cited the school data and some of the characteristics of the school (see Tables 2.1 and 2.2) in their 1996 inspection report.

Table 2.1 Pupil data – Gladstone Street Primary School

	Number of pupils on roll (full-time equivalent)	Number of pupils with statements of SEN	Number of pupils on school's register of SEN	Number of full-time pupils eligible for free school meals
YR–Y6	274	3	45	70 (25%)

Table 2.2 Teachers and classes – Gladstone Street Primary School

Total number of qualified teachers	13
Number of pupils per qualified teacher	21
Average class size	27
Average teaching group size	28

Table 2.3 Details of staff joining or leaving Gladstone Street Primary School during or after special measures

Name	Age	Responsibility	Key stage	Date joining or leaving	If left school – reason	Interviewed
Colin	54	Headteacher	1 & 2	March 1997	Voluntary resignation	✓
Gerri	41	Finance	N/A	March 1999	Voluntary resignation	
Amy	42	Librarian	N/A	December 1998	Redundancy	
Lance	32	Classroom assistant	1	March 1999	Redundancy	
Veronica	42	Deputy headteacher	1 & 2	January 1999	N/A	✓
Rita	44	Teacher	1 & 2	December 1998	Voluntary resignation	✓
Vanessa	49	Teacher	2	April 1998	Transfer to another school	✓
Rebecca	48	Deputy headteacher	1 & 2	April 1998	Voluntary resignation	
Janice	58	Teacher	2	August 1996	Early retirement	
Edith	33	Teacher	2	December 1996	Voluntary resignation	✓
Melanie	28	Teacher	1	July 1998	Transfer to another school	
Priscilla	45	Teacher	2	September 1999	N/A	
Ivor	38	Teacher	2	November 1998	N/A	
Juliette	25	Teacher	2	January 1998	N/A	✓
Catherine	49	Teacher	1	April 1998	N/A	✓
Anthony	42	Headteacher	1 & 2	March 1998	N/A	✓
Andy	52	Site manager	N/A	March 1999	N/A	
Sean	45	KS 1 Co-ordinator	1	January 1997	N/A	✓
George	45	Teacher	2	March 1996	Voluntary resignation	✓
Kathy	40	Maths Co-ordinator	2	March 1997	Voluntary resignation	✓

Table 2.4 Teachers working at Gladstone Street Primary School before, during and after special measures

Name	Age	Responsibility	Key stage	Interviewed
Frances	55	0.5 Section 11 Teacher	1 & 2	✔
Geraldine	30	Art Co-ordinator	2	✔
Joan	50	English Co-ordinator	2	✔
Richard	40	Science, IT and Games Co-ordinator		✔
Maisie	55	0.5 Section 11 Teacher		✔

The main school opened in 1967 on the site of the original Victorian building. A fee-paying playgroup, subsidised by the local authority, opened in 1995. Most children in the current intake have attended local playgroups or nursery classes prior to entry. Their attainment on entry is wide, but broadly average, and contains roughly equal numbers of boys and girls. The pupils come from a wide range of backgrounds, 49 per cent are from ethnic minority families, and most of these are supported through Section 11 funding. 16 per cent of the pupils are identified as requiring additional support of whom 1 per cent have statements of SEN, this is below the national average. 40 per cent of pupils come from out of the catchment area.

Details of the staff joining or leaving during and after special measures are shown in Table 2.3.

Details of teachers who also currently work at the school and taught there before the inspection who were interviewed are shown in Table 2.4.

After failing its Ofsted inspection the school spent two years in special measures. During this period, the headteacher at the time of the inspection, Colin Jones, resigned from his post. He was succeeded by a seconded headteacher from the LEA. After one term she was replaced by another headteacher on secondment who was in post for a term before the appointment of the current headteacher, Anthony Edwards, during the final term of special measures. Of the thirteen full-time teachers at the time of the inspection, eight, including the deputy headteacher, left the school during the period spent in special measures.

Geoff spent one week in the school early in the term following its removal from special measures. Data was collected in the form of observational notes and tape-recorded interviews. The semi-structured interviews, carried out with the teachers, were generally of one hour's duration. Transcripts of the interviews were analysed using theme analysis and the constant comparative method (Glaser and Strauss, 1967). Colin Jones and five of the teachers who had left the school at various stages during the special measures period were also interviewed. Colin described some of these staff changes as follows:

The deputy's gone, a senior member of staff, the one that was in year six went with me. We taught together for years. One teacher retired immediately after the Ofsted. I asked her to stay on for an extra term although she asked to go beforehand, and died three months later of stomach cancer. And a couple of other members of staff have finished. So the fallout – both short and long term – has been enormous.

The Gladstone Street ethos: caring and sharing

Before the Ofsted inspection in 1996, Gladstone Street was characterised by strongly positive emotions, centred on caring and sharing. The school prioritised human relationships (cf. Nias et al., 1992). Many of the staff had chosen to come to the school for the psychic and social rewards (Lortie, 1975; Rosenholtz, 1989) it offered. It was described by teachers as a child-centred and multicultural school that had developed excellent community relations.

Richard had come to teach at the school at a 'very turbulent time' in his personal life and found the school a 'haven' and the 'only stable part of my life at the time'. Colin described the school as an 'oasis' and emotionally as an 'asphalt *Cinderella*'. Edith liked the 'very close knit and supportive staff'. Frances felt, 'there was such a good atmosphere in the school and people were very caring about the children, the needs of the children and about each other'. Colin found it

> difficult to avoid almost an emotional terminology when I try to describe what we were about, I believe that was so shared by the other folk, although you'd need to ask them about that. But teachers when they joined us stayed because teaching at this school can get under your skin.

Colin remained at the school for the 'buzz' he got from developing sound community links:

> I was so happy at Gladstone Street that after being effective for five years. I was thinking about the next move, a second headship. I couldn't think of anywhere else I'd rather be and there was so much to be done, especially in terms of grounds development and community links being developed and forged. But nothing else took my eye and I continued to work away within what I regarded as a very special and privileged community. And I'm in no doubt that the personal buzz I got through being regarded almost in a rather old-fashioned way as a centre of that particular hub of activity, and the great deal of time and attention given to me by the various community leaders, that psychologically I got a tremendous ego boost being part of that particular little empire.

He was confirmed in his values and approaches partly by the school being able to attract some middle class children from out of the area:

> There was a hard core of what one might call middle or upper class parents who, because of the work we were doing and their liberal or even socialist attitudes towards society and education generally had elected to put their children in our school, including the local MP and two headteachers. Twenty other teachers within the city had their children at our school and this gave us the clue that we actually should be on the right lines, otherwise these professional parents who were observing us would have spotted it. I had no negative feedback from any of those folk at all. And I used them – albeit subconsciously – as a yardstick for our progress. So there was this – I call it a hard core – but in fact it was a substantial number of articulate, university lecturing folk and serving teachers, secondary and primary, who were the back-bone of the PTA; the governing board. And, as I say, my yardstick for being on the right lines.
>
> We were proud of what we were doing within our community and the hard work that we were putting into both the educational delivery and all the other emotional, social and physical factors that go to make up a school community. We would sing our own praises to anyone who cared to listen and make the point frequently that 40 per cent of our intake were out of area, which we thought was significant of the popularity of the school and the standing that we had in, not only the local, but more far reaching communities.

Edith pointed to the fact that the urban context of the school and range of children attending attracted teachers who liked a challenge:

> At that time this was generally thought to be a fairly challenging school to teach in just because of the sheer mix of children. I don't know whether the catchment area has changed but at that time we had some very bright children from educated homes who were very motivated and some children with huge problems, really devastating social problems. And then of course we had quite a high proportion of bilingual learners which I saw as an exciting and positive thing but it does make teaching more challenging in a way because you have to be constantly thinking about getting the message across to a range of children, rather than just aiming at a mid point. There's such a range of minds to reach in that situation.

A child-centred ethos was maintained at the school despite a national atmosphere that was becoming more curriculum and standards centred. Colin summed up the ethos:

We attempted to recognise the individuality of each of our youngsters. But looking back I suppose we were flying in the face of the cold wind that was blowing then, that everybody should be pushed along the same educational channel and the pupil sausages would be popping out at the other end as neatly as *Wall's* could do it in their real sausage factory.

Sean agreed:

They come to school with so much potential. All these young kids; these three and four year olds. They've got so much individuality already. I see in other schools and with other reception class teachers that are being just ignored. They're just crammed in. The first lesson they have to learn is that they're just a small part of a big system.

He viewed the teachers at Gladstone Street as being able to form good relationships with the children:

I would like to think that everybody here has some added part of their personality, the part of them which actually brings some individual colour to what they do as opposed to just being a technician. Most of the people who are working here actually like kids. I know some teachers who ... don't like children, they don't know how to speak to children, they don't know how to relate to children.... Maybe those sort of people will coast through as technicians because they see the people they are working with just as people who have to go through the hoops of what they're asking them to do. But I don't think there's anybody here like that. I get the feeling that most people actually enjoy working with children and enjoy the actual spark of being around young people as they're learning.

Anthony identified multiculturalism, an emphasis on individuality, emotional development and caring as important aspects of life at the school:

They (teachers) are very much of a professional group of people who see an important part of school life as being a celebration of our cultural diversity, putting the child first. So we're a child-centred school and a person centred school so that the individuals with different viewpoints, we'll build our structure around those people. They want to see good pastoral care, they want to see – well basically it's about emotional literacy. They want to see children being dealt with appropriately and being taught to deal with their own problems. It's about formation and growth.

Edith was much happier at Gladstone Street than at her previous school because:

This seemed like a school that was much more focused on the children and I felt much more in sympathy with the school ethos. I'd found at the previous school that things like the issue of bilingual learners were completely swept under the carpet and I felt I wasn't able to help those children as much as I would have liked to. Whereas here it was much more in the foreground of people's thinking. There was much more tolerance of children with difficult home backgrounds and sympathy for them which was much more in keeping with my feelings about how children should be dealt with. And I didn't feel quite so much like somebody with minority ideas really. And I found the head supportive here.

Anthony explained the school's popularity with the LEA, parents, children and teachers:

The school was held as a bit of a beacon around the city. The head-teacher was a good man who was good in the sense that the pastoral care and the ethos and the community base of the school were excellent, second to none really. And he was always praising his teachers.

The inspection

The inspection completely transformed the picture. Edith had felt confident before the inspection because 'it was well known that this school was doing fine'. Colin too felt very confident about the school's inspection prospects even though he was entering the process without his deputy who suffered a breakdown in the build-up to the inspection week:

In the late eighties and throughout the nineties the work got harder. Social problems increased. Our determination to face them and deal with them first and foremost and then try and attend to the reforms that had been foisted upon us, led to a fair amount of teacher stress before Ofsted came along. But we were so confident in that what we were doing was right and successful and couldn't possibly be gainsaid by any other lucid and right thinking person, that I fully expected, along with my colleagues, except for one, the crucial deputy head, that we would not only sail through Ofsted but be commended for the extra efforts that we were making.

Indeed, Ofsted acknowledged these caring and sharing aspects as strengths of the school in their inspection report. However, the school was judged to be failing because of: poor leadership and management; poor financial management (including a budget deficit and not providing value for money); poor pupil behaviour; teachers' low expectations of the pupils; and poor teaching quality. During the inspection week Colin realised that things were 'rapidly going pear shaped' and 'shockingly wrong' and tried to retrieve the situation by trying to demonstrate that, although SATs scores were low when compared to national averages, the school had 'added value' to its pupils:

> He (Registered Inspector) really did work hard to get up the noses of some of the staff – not myself. The only thing he did which I'll never forgive him for was on the very last day, the Friday, when I was trying to rescue the situation by providing evidence that the SATs indicated that we had made at least average progress. While I was in my final passionate rescue speech with these two guys, I'd called in early to see them, he looked at his watch twice and that to me was a symbol of the fact that the guy was callous and it wasn't going to make any difference.

Anthony felt that prior to the failure the school had a deficit view of the children that neglected serious issues concerning the school's role in raising educational achievement:

> There was this acceptance that the area the school is in is a hard place to live and be, that our children are always from the lower end of the learning spectrum. We have a high proportion of bilingual children and therefore our achievements academically will always be a struggle for us. And if you just go round the school, that's obvious in the neglect of the buildings. So there's something there. But unfortunately with KS 2 SATs and KS 1 SATs and league tables you couldn't hide behind that kind of impression anymore because it would come out and be made public.

Joan succinctly stated Ofsted's reasons for failing the school:

> I think that the staff are very caring. One thing we got criticised for in Ofsted was that we cared at the expense of education. Too busy nurturing, not enough time educating.

And Richard recognised that responding to the recommendations in the report would involve making a major change to the school's aims and ethos:

> We had to change priorities and had to completely re-focus our energies from pastoral care and then education to education and pastoral care.

There might be doubts about the soundness of the Ofsted judgement – Ofsted does not have a high reputation among academics for the validity of its findings (Fitz-Gibbon, 1996; Wilcox and Gray, 1996; Jeffrey and

Woods, 1998). However, leaving that question aside, assuming even that they may have been right, was placing the school in 'special measures' the best way to proceed to secure 'improvement'?

The emotions of failure

There is growing evidence and realisation that emotions are a central aspect of teaching (Nias, 1996; Hargreaves, 1998c and 1999a). Hargreaves (1998c: 835), for example, claims that 'good teaching is charged with positive emotions'. He has in mind the passion and enthusiasm that teachers bring to their work, their search for fun and excitement in teaching and learning, the emotional bonds they form with their students and their fellow teachers, their drive for new challenges and new experiences. 'Teaching', says Hargreaves, 'cannot be reduced to technical competence or clinical standards' (ibid.: 850). However, this does not appear to be the view currently of government or of Ofsted. There is no emotional understanding, whereby one 'enters into the field of experience of another and experiences for oneself the same or similar experiences experienced by another' (Denzin, 1984: 137). There is little appreciation of the emotional labour (Hochschild, 1993) engaged in by teachers, the work they put in to make learning meaningful to their students, but which also makes them vulnerable 'when the conditions of and demands on their work make it hard for them to do their "emotion work" properly' (Hargreaves, 1998c: 840). Rather, teachers become involved in emotional politics (Blase and Anderson, 1995) as they wrestle with countervailing and superior forces. Our case study portrays the negative impact this had on teachers.

Shock

The teachers experienced a great emotional shock during the inspection week when they realised they were failing. This was reinforced by the announcement that the school had failed and they were to be placed in special measures. Joan explained that it was 'a total shock nobody had expected – it just hit me – my whole life was affected – it was a horrible time'. Richard said 'the atmosphere was hysterical – people were crushed – everyone was stripped raw – the teachers were crumbling'. Colin explained:

> Such was our thinking at the time that this couldn't possibly happen and we were in such a state of shock that it was difficult to respond. People used images such as we were rabbits caught in the headlights of a car.

Frances said 'the foundations of the school had been kicked hard'.

The reality of failure had come as even more of a shock, because, in addition to the many indications of the school's success discussed earlier,

Gladstone Street had had a very successful LEA pre-inspection monitoring visit. Not only was the school given what Sean described as 'a clean bill of health', but was viewed by a senior LEA inspector as a 'beacon of good practice' by the authority. Sean explained that this inspector had subsequently 'washed his hands of the school'. Richard's sense of shock was accompanied by anger over what he saw as 'being lied to by the LEA inspector'.

To assist the staff who were experiencing 'anger, disbelief and numbness' (Richard), and who had been 'blown apart' and were 'like zombies', Colin bought in the services of some disaster counsellors experienced in supporting people with post-traumatic stress disorder. They ran two group therapy sessions with the whole staff.

We might note the functionality of shock. The inspectors might claim that this is what is needed in order to disabuse teachers of taken-for-grantedness, to shake them out of old and outmoded ways of thinking, and to create space for new thinking, all in the interests of driving up educational standards and school improvement. However, in cutting the ground from under teachers' feet Ofsted induced a state of anomie with the only outlet offered a narrow technicist path. The broader aspects of teachers' expertise were put at risk because they were not valued so highly. This induced feelings of guilt and shame among the teachers.

Shame

The most prominent feeling among our teachers was one of shame. Giddens (1991: 65) comments that 'some argue that guilt is a private anxiety state, shame is a public one'. He cites the example of Sartre who 'treats shame as a visible phenomenon giving as an example a man who makes a vulgar gesture – he then realises he is being observed; seeing himself suddenly through the eyes of the other he feels shame' (ibid.). Anthony explained that:

> I'm sure that the teachers felt really badly let down by the management because they had all this extra pressure and extra work and guilt and shame. And I don't use those words lightly, I really mean that. The level of shame in those early days of failing schools was considerable. Because this school was the first one to fail. A secondary school had failed but we were the first primary or junior school to fail here. Genuine guilt and shame came not necessarily because they were bad teachers but because they were badly led teachers.

Their failure, then, was highly visible and took place at the time the media were searching for the 'worst school in Britain' and 'Sun-style headlines – "Failing School Named: Incompetent Teachers to be Sacked" – were strident in their simplifying terror' (Ball, 1998: 78).

Colin, anticipating hostile media coverage, managed to delay publication of the report findings in the local media and requested secrecy from the teachers lest leaks were reported:

> I had to rescue the traumatised groups and the school from collapsing from the other side. And we knew that the press would get hold of this and the only sympathetic act from the inspection team was the agreement to sit on the report until the middle of August so that we could at least have a break during the summer and get our act together before a press conference near the end of August, so that when the report was issued in early September we were ready with our responses. So we massaged the media as best we could as a damage limitation exercise although we knew that we would be front page of the local press and we were. And the radio. So my job was to stop people running naked down the road, if I can use that image.

Anthony said that after publication of the report 'the school was hammered by the media'.

Giddens (1991: 65) argues that 'shame depends on feelings of personal insufficiency' and 'should be understood in relation to the integrity of the self, while guilt derives from feelings of wrongdoing'. For Lewis (1971, cited in Giddens, 1991: 65), shame comes from 'the unconsciously expressed anxieties about inadequacies of the self' and leads to feelings of psychological insecurity and fears that 'the narrative of the self-identity cannot withstand engulfing pressures on its coherence or social acceptability. Shame eats at the roots of trust more corrosively than guilt'. Whereas shame is negative, the opposite emotions are positive, and involve pride, self-esteem, and confidence in the integrity and value of the self (Giddens, 1991: 65).

The teachers' experience of psychological insecurity and inadequacy induced by shame were visible, and feelings of inadequacy were preceded by the onset of self-doubt. The teachers questioned their accumulated knowledge and experience of schools and teaching. Sean felt that the school's failing had 'brought everything into question'. Joan thought:

> It was that total confusion because people couldn't believe that some of their colleagues had been criticised. People they thought were good teachers. It was just a total muddle really.

Edith felt her 'judgement had all gone wrong' and 'found it difficult to evaluate if (she) was a good teacher or not'. Ann, who had considerable experience as a support teacher and had worked in the classrooms of many colleagues over the years was 'shocked because I thought I knew what teaching was. It made me question if I knew anything about teaching at all even though I had a lot of experience to judge'. Richard wondered if he had 'chosen the wrong career'. While some of the teachers had been informed of the quality of their teaching by the inspectors and others had discerned evaluations of themselves from the inspection report others had to rely on other means of finding out. Kathy, for instance, thought her teaching competence would be affirmed in the grading system for teaching but then found out that:

> In that inspection you weren't told personally, you didn't have any feedback about your teaching. So you didn't know whether you'd just missed being an excellent teacher. Because if you had a grade one or two they had to tell you because that meant you were very, very good. And if you had a six or seven then you were pretty awful. And unless you were one of those you weren't told. So you didn't know whether you'd just escaped being the most brilliant teacher there was or whether you'd just scraped through and were pretty awful really.

Edith did not think she was a 'total disaster' but was not 'altogether sure'. Richard did not know whether he should accept Ofsted's evaluation of him as a 'failed teacher' as:

> The headteacher had sat down and identified all the positives that were in the report and we already knew all the negatives. But some of the positives were wrong as well. What they had identified as being things that were working well in the school they obviously hadn't looked at closely enough because they were not working properly. We knew they weren't working properly. So if that was true of the positives, what was it saying about some of the negatives? One of the thoughts going through my head was, 'how true is their assessment of what's happened?'

Goffman (1952: 454) argues that:

> The moment of failure often catches a person acting as one who feels that he [sic] is an appropriate sort of person for the role in question. Assumption becomes presumption, and failure becomes fraud.

This situation seems to have been anticipated by Edith:

> I just didn't want people looking at me. I had this feeling that if anybody looked at my planning books or in my files or if anybody looked at me teaching they'd find out what a fraud I really was.

Teachers that had managed to find out Ofsted's evaluation of them started comparing themselves with their colleagues. This 'social comparing' (Crace, 1999a) resulted in some teachers finding out that their colleagues had done much better than them. This tended to lower their already low self-esteem. This was particularly acute for Richard who hadn't liked being 'lumped in with all the other failing teachers', and whose wife taught at the school and had been judged to be a successful teacher.

Colin retired prematurely with very strong feelings of self-doubt about his professional abilities:

> I had a tremendous inner conflict between what the external judgement had made on my managerial competency, although they actually steered clear of criticising me directly. It all came down to what was happening in the classroom for which I was ultimately responsible of course. So there is an element of falling on swords here. But such were my feelings of 'Could they have been right?' Here is this huge government edifice that is designed to give a fair report after thousands of pounds have been spent on creating the opportunity to look carefully at the school. Could they possibly be wrong? And, therefore, was I fit for the job? That was one imp on my shoulder. And on the other side was a voice that said, 'You are very knowledgeable about your skill base and your competency and what you got from other people around you'. It gave me a strong message that actually I could hack it. I was only fifty-two, so I'd made plans to pull away from what was an almost intolerably stressful job by the age of fifty-six anyway. So I brought that forward. Otherwise it would have killed me.

Again, from Ofsted's point of view, this is perfectly functional. They had diagnosed a management problem. It was solved at a stroke. But the brutal cure had embraced more than its target.

Inadequacy

As argued earlier, shame involves experiencing feelings of inadequacy. Sean felt that whereas before the inspection he used to 'feel quite a good teacher' the experience of failure had resulted in what he felt was an 'erosion of personal skills'. Ofsted had found 'skills missing' in Richard's practice and he felt 'A complete failure – I didn't think I had a future in teaching.' Frances said, 'We were lacking in confidence; a lack of confidence in our abilities. Always checking things, and re-checking.'

Even some of those teachers judged to be successful felt acutely inadequate, like Vanessa:

> I had taught an excellent lesson or a very good lesson on the first day and they have to tell you when you teach a very good lesson. And the Ofsted inspector came in the next day. We were so out of touch with how our teaching was and everybody was so utterly stressed, I was convinced that he was going to tell me that I taught a failing lesson and I could feel myself going. And he was going through his huge file saying, 'We're required by law to tell teachers, inform teachers, if they

teach very bad lessons or very good lessons and because we're required by law I have to tell you that –'. So he actually led up in a way that was utterly stressful. He didn't give any indication whether it was going to be failing or good and he said 'and I'm pleased to tell you that the lesson I observed yesterday was a 1' or whatever it was.

Some of the teachers with good personal reports felt a strong collegiate responsibility and experienced collective inadequacy. Edith found the inspection

> so awful. I think it was because there was this strong feeling here of being part of a team and I didn't feel that I could say, 'Oh well, they said my teaching was sound so that's OK'. Because I'd been part of all the policy making and the discussions about which way the school was going and I think there was a fairly common feeling about how we should approach the education of the children at this school. And I'd been part of that. So the comment about the teaching in year one was the only one that could be related to me personally but it seemed only one thing amongst many that I'd been part of. I identified with the school sufficiently to feel criticised by the general criticism of the school.

Joan was anxious lest her potential personal failure would affect her colleagues negatively:

> I was really, really scared, because I had one of the big-wig inspectors watching a Science lesson. I thought, 'Oh God! I've got "good" so far! This is going to be one where I don't get a good report, and I'll let everybody down.'

Anthony was concerned in case the 'succeeding' teachers were 'dragged down' by the failing ones. A temporary headteacher who was not respected by the teachers had adopted top-down management strategies which increased feelings of inadequacy in the teachers:

> JOAN: I was at a meeting and somebody told me this head had said that he was put here to kick arse, I think that was his expression. So instead of telling people just what was found in the report, he picked up on anything negative and threw it back at them. And he was saying, 'Get your act together or you're not going to get out of special measures'.
>
> FRANCES: And basically told us that we were no good, that we were impolite, that we'd got a reputation for being nice but we weren't. He threw all this at us at one staff meeting. We were too weakened to respond.

JOAN: I think people resented him coming in for a term and telling us (who'd been through hell and back) that we were still not making the grade and what were we going to do about it. And he came in with the attitude that we were all failures, all rubbish.

The experience of repeated inspections by HMI and LEA inspectors during special measures, although confidence building for some teachers (see later), completely undermined others' sense of efficacy and adequacy. Rita, for example, felt that she was:

Such a useless lump; you're not a good teacher. You're a waste of time and space. And it sort of feeds on itself really. So your confidence is just hacked away. You feel inside yourself that what you need is constructive criticism. You can always find something to be constructive about in a lesson. Nobody does everything wrong, you can always find something that is being done right. But it always seemed to me that this person – this particular person – was always looking for the worst and never looking to give credit where there was some credit due. And the longer it went on the less confidence I had.

Edith felt so inadequate that she totally lacked confidence in situations which demanded it:

The thing that began to really worry me was that things would happen with children with difficult behaviour and I would find myself kind of frozen. I didn't know what to do – I couldn't think how to react to it. And that was a bad sign. In fact when I told my dad about it he said that it really worried him that I was feeling like that. And when I left (resigned), he said that he was very glad that I had. He said, 'I think you would have had a nervous breakdown if you'd carried on'. I'm very relieved now I've left.

The stigma of failure

Goffman (1952: 461) argues that:

A person is an individual who becomes involved in a value of some kind – a role, a status, a relationship, an ideology – and then makes a public claim that he [sic] is to be defined and treated as someone who possesses the value or property in question. The limits to his claims, and hence the limits to his self, are primarily determined by the objective facts of his social life and secondarily determined by the degree to which a sympathetic interpretation of these facts can bend them in his favour. Any event which demonstrates that someone has made a false claim, defining himself as something which he is not, tends to destroy him. If others realize that the person's conception of self has been contradicted and discredited, then the person tends to be destroyed in the eyes of others.

Snow and Anderson (1987: 1339) argue that 'our most basic drive is for a sense of self-worth or personal significance and that its accessibility depends in part on the roles available to us'. Many kinds of work, particularly professional work such as teaching, can provide 'role-based sources of moral worth and dignity for the individual' (ibid.). Those who have failed bear a stigma; a stain on their reputation. The fear of stigmatisation, therefore, adds to feelings of inadequacy and threatens the individual's sense of self-worth and dignity.

Kathy, for example, encountered stigmatisation from the LEA inspector who had given the school a good report prior to failure by Ofsted and didn't appear to have any strategies to manage the situation, other than to turn his back on it:

> During the summer holidays I was up in the town and saw one of the LEA advisers who was closely connected with the school so he knew me as Kathy, I knew him. And I saw him coming up the road towards me and I suppose I was feeling a bit tender as it were after all this and I said 'Oh hello' and he said 'Hello' and turned his head and walked on. And I felt that was a bit of a slight and I thought perhaps he deliberately ignored me because normally you would say, 'Have a good holiday', or something like that, and then I put that out of my mind. But he'd run this particular course that was on that day in October and he'd done something I'd particularly noticed. I'd sat at the back of the room and other people had come in and they'd say to me, 'Sorry to hear your bad news', and this sort of thing. And the entire afternoon he'd looked at everybody else but he didn't look at me and he didn't acknowledge me at all. And I did feel very hurt about this. And I felt that – because he had been in and said we were fine. He'd been in and seen all my assessment records and said everything was fine. And I'd felt that he'd dissociated himself from failure. And I began to feel that I just didn't want to be associated with people like this any more, who could do this to such a school, who could actually destroy the school, because this is what I felt he'd done.

The stress of failure

Although symptoms of stress are clear in the teachers' testimonies cited so far, there were further indicators. Some teachers, though not experiencing stress-related illness, became 'stressed at seeing colleagues go under and extremely angry at seeing what the system has done to others' (Sean). Frances became stressed because a colleague with whom she worked collaboratively and who was also a close friend was absent from school owing to a nervous breakdown. Quite apart from the extra work involved, Frances had to cope with the emotional strain. Colin was on his 'knees physically and emotionally, and ground down by it all'. Anthony said many teachers were 'exhausted and couldn't keep working at that pace; they were on a stress-ridden downward path; and stress levels were high and morale was low'. Sean experienced sleeplessness prior to the termly inspections:

> I got a lot of sleepless nights as well thinking about a lesson and turning it over and over in my head. And every tiny component of a lesson; when the inspector was coming in; every word I would say. And that doesn't make for a good lesson. It makes you really nervous and it makes it much harder to work properly with the children.

Frances explained that the staff responded emotionally throughout special measures:

> I couldn't stop crying. I couldn't talk about school without crying all the time. After Anthony arrived things calmed down so much and I said to a friend of mine I hadn't realised how bad it sounded, it shows things have got so much better. I don't think I've cried at school this term. Before, a lot of us were crying; anything would set you off.

Richard experienced depression:

> I'd just been getting more and more depressed. I just got tireder and tireder and tireder. And it didn't matter how much I slept I always thought if I get an extra half hour's sleep I'll feel fine. But I never got that extra half-hour's sleep. And even when I did I didn't feel any better. I had the summer off, came back to work, within two weeks I was exhausted. That's mid September for God's sake. You think, 'What's this job doing to me'. And I spent another couple of months beavering away. I'd made the decision to kind of come in particularly early so I was coming in at seven. I decided just because it was light I would leave at five, so I was working a ten hour day, every day. I was spending most of my Sunday working. I started to feel as though I was able to get some control back. Because before it just felt as though everything was out of my hands. It was just sliding away from me. And I've been able to take back a lot of the control. I can still feel myself kind of a bit shaky and there are tears at the back of my eyes just waiting for the right kind of poke to come out. And when we actually came out of special measures I wasn't elated. I was probably a bit relieved. But my wife put it quite well she said, 'It's a couple of years and they've stopped beating you up now, and it's relief that they've stopped doing that but it still hurts; you still feel sore'.

The feelings of hopelessness and despair; emotional and physical exhaustion; tearfulness and crying; low self-esteem; feelings of worthlessness, inadequacy and of being out of control; self-doubt; loss of confidence; and anxiety, all evident in the accounts of these teachers are all classic symptoms of depression (Wolpert, 1999). While it is not possible to demonstrate causality from these data (or indeed, any form of data) there does seem to be a strong positive correlation between the onset of stress and depression and the teachers' experience of failure and subsequent working in special measures. While the 'causes' of depression undoubtedly involve biological (genetic), psychological and social factors it 'always occurs in a social context' (Wolpert, 1999: 51). Sources of depression are, therefore, multi-factorial. 'Relationships, work, poverty, hopes, children, parents and so on can all play some role in the generation of a depressive episode' (ibid). Much work on depression has focused on the significance of 'life events' in the generation of depression. These are 'stressful external changes that are rapid, even sudden, and whose time of occurrence can be given a clear and specific date' (ibid). School failure and special measures must count as significant life events in this case study as it seems no coincidence that of the eight teachers to leave the school after its failure and during the period of special measures that at least four of these were professionally diagnosed as suffering from clinical depression.

Managing failure and shame

Failure and shame are socially produced. Individuals experiencing these states devise strategies to manage the self and social processes contributing to their experience of negative emotions, thus attempting to mitigate the impact of failure and resultant shame. The teachers used strategies of *personal adjustment or departure*; *stigma management*; some *rationalised* failure and shame while others *transcended* them.

Personal adjustment or departure

The majority of those teachers suffering from stress or depression left the school (some leaving teaching altogether) at a relatively early stage in special measures. Colin was a paradigm case of this form of exit. Others, however, continued and during special measures suffered physically and emotionally under pressures from management to change and improve their practice and repeated inspections by HMI and LEA inspectors. Ofsted recognise this kind of situation and recommend the following:

> Those whose teaching has been judged to be unsatisfactory are not necessarily poor teachers who are incapable of improving. It may be that they have suffered from weak management of the school, so their teaching problems have not been identified and relevant in-service

training has not been provided. This group of teachers can and should be helped to improve their teaching. Many teachers who were once weak have become consistently sound at their job once they have understood what needs to be done and been helped to do it – indeed, some have become very good teachers. Other teachers cannot, or do not wish to, change their ways of working. In such cases, the school should not shy away from removing staff who cannot fulfil their responsibilities as teachers. While the school carries staff who are not pulling their weight, teaching standards cannot be improved overall, and pupils will continue to suffer.

Sean was successfully 'changed' by the newly appointed headteacher, Anthony:

> He would actually fight against the process of producing better academic standards which was necessary to get out of special measures. His personal philosophy wouldn't allow for it. So I approached it from two issues really. One is I came in with a mandate of we're going to move forward with the academic standards like it or not, and you either come with me or we'll have to go into whatever procedures are needed to make you come over. But it is going to happen. So I set my stall up very early on. But the other thing was to actually spend some time with him, quite a few hours talking through why he believed what he believed, what right had he to impinge that personal philosophy on a group of children and their families who might actually have very different philosophies, and also what right had he to pass classes up to future teachers that hadn't had their National Curriculum entitlement. Whatever he personally believed he was working in the system and getting paid a hell of a lot of money, on a point eleven as head of KS 1, to actually do his job. Now if he didn't like his job he needs to go and find another one. Now I had no problem with that. What I had a problem with was his not doing the job which he was being paid to do.

That some teachers should change or be removed was seen clearly by some of the teachers. However, Joan commented:

> I think that's what Ofsted set out to do. Figures show, don't they, that in most schools that get out of special measures, first the head goes, and quite often the deputy goes, and they do have a turnover of staff.

Here the emphasis is on teachers leaving rather than improving. In practice Joan saw the following process being enacted:

You have some inspections that are announced and you have some that are unannounced. And you only have a matter of weeks and if you don't do what they want you to do in that inspection time then you just get the push basically.

Talking about a specific case, Rita, Joan said:

She knew it would eventually come to competency procedures. The awful thing was that there was a point where you couldn't tell if she couldn't cope with it because she couldn't adapt or if she couldn't cope with it because she was very stressed.

This indicates the complexity of the situation in which a stressed teacher is attempting to respond to change. The situation is further complicated by knowing that Joan thought Rita to be a good teacher. Not only was Rita a personal friend but Joan was happy to have her children taught by her. Indeed Rita was a godparent of her daughter. But this view of Rita was not shared by all of the teachers, such as Vanessa:

I hate to sound unkind but I think possibly some of the people who left teaching should have left teaching. That sounds vindictive but I think teachers have to be flexible. I think they have to stay current. And if you're not prepared to do that then I don't think you should be a teacher. Having said that I think it's grossly unfair for teachers who are really keen to do well, work really hard and through no fault of their own don't make the grade. I feel really, really sad for Rita. I knew it was on the cards, I knew that she would be the next person they'd be going for. And I didn't want to be here. I saw what they did to Angela. That was the right thing to do but it was such an un-pleasant process. She wasn't actually present in the school during Ofsted because she was off with stress – basically I think she had a nervous breakdown. And she came back after Ofsted and basically couldn't cope I don't think. And because of the position she was in, she wasn't teaching well, she wasn't coping well, the appraisals were showing that up and we just saw her disintegrate. She just went from bad to worse. And it was a very unpleasant thing to be around. And then I could see the writing on the wall with Rita. And Rita drives me nuts. But she's great. She works really hard, she tries really hard, and I could just see the writing on the wall. I could just see they were going to start hounding her, dismantling her confidence and didn't want to see that really.

The teachers leaving the school were, in the main, older, more experienced and thus more expensive. Like the corporate downsizing in the business sector of the 1980s and 1990s, staff reductions are a rapid means of reversing budget deficits. Indeed, this strategy of financial recovery for the failing school is advocated by Ofsted (1999: 52).

Managing stigma

There are a 'variety of strategies frequently used by the stigmatised to minimise the deleterious social and psychic consequences of their discrediting attributes' (Snow and Anderson, 1987: 1339). These involve engaging in 'identity work' in order to manage a 'spoiled identity' (Goffman, 1963).

Thus, Richard was expecting to be stigmatised by colleagues in the authority and used the strategy of 'concealing or withholding information about the stigma so that it was not easily perceived by others' (Snow and Anderson, 1987: 1339):

> And I got on and I went along to this course and I was so bloody embarrassed. I didn't want anyone to know. I used to say I was a teacher, I used to say things like, 'Oh I work in a school in the city'. And then over the week they kind of narrowed it down until eventually I did actually tell people I came from Gladstone Street. And they said, 'It must have been so hard for you'. And whereas I thought they would just smirk and snigger and walk away, they didn't at all. They were – not incredibly supportive – but there was just some kind of sympathy if not empathy for what the whole school had gone through.

Edith did not want to face the stigmatisation potentially resulting from having taught at a failing school. She felt knowledge of the fact of failure and her stress would deter a potential employer who might think she was a 'lousy teacher from a failing school'. She wondered 'who would employ someone like me'. She did not want to take extended sick leave because:

> If I had a long time off work I would find it very difficult to get a different job. I panicked really. I thought well if I want to get employment in another field I need to be able to present it as a cool, calm decision. Which I mean looking back it wasn't at all. And it probably didn't come across that way. But I was desperate not to be kind of invalided out really.

During her interview for a different occupation she anticipated the stigmatisation of stress and failure and managed the questioning in what she clearly thought was a skilful way:

> I think I got off very lightly in that because they asked me – and I guess it's all part of employment practices – they work out their questions very carefully. They asked me what I liked and what I disliked about my last job. And I was canny enough to present it in positive

terms. I told them what I liked about it but I presented what I disliked about it in a way that was likely to be positive in terms of the new job. I told them that I disliked the fact that there was such an extreme pressure of work that it wasn't possible to do things thoroughly, which is true. But I'd already grasped enough about what would be required of me in my new job to realise that they wouldn't actually want me to be capable of taking a lot of responsibility but they would want me to be thorough. So I suppose I twisted it around to be in my favour in that situation.

Colin found it necessary to employ strategies to deal with the media in order to try and salvage not only his reputation but also the school's:

If we had responded as we ought to have done and said, 'this is shit and wrong', we'd have had the *Daily Mail* on our doorstep. You can imagine the headline: 'Labour MP's children at Failed School'. You can write your own headlines and that would have done the school down and we would have had awful publicity. So we had to subjugate our feelings about being treated unfairly and go with the flow to give lip service to the fact that all the phrases had to be churned out and give an airing to the press about how we were going to work hard to put right the factors that had been identified. But in our heart of hearts we knew that the matters that had been identified were false. But there wasn't any other way round that. There's no appeal and we would have done damage to the school if we'd done things any differently.

Rationalising failure and shame

Those who have experienced failure can 'develop explanations and excuses to account in a creditable way for their failure' (Goffman, 1952: 459). Colin reacted to the school's and his personal failure by claiming that Ofsted's verdict had been a 'travesty; a miscarriage of justice'. While recognising that he was constructing a conspiracy theory he saw the local political situation in the authority and the following details of the conduct of the inspection to be instrumental in the failure:

There were various bits of evidence that the new Registered Inspector who was an ex-HMI down from the North was a personal friend of the CEO. Bits and pieces like this that added to the conspiracy theory and that in a way he was going for us. All heads within the country had been warned that inspection teams were now rooting to find and to fail at KS 2 wherever they could. Because there'd been only a few failures and it meant that Ofsted actually weren't demonstrating they had any teeth. You can't actually create an edifice that's powerful and influential unless there is this bottom line of a punishment strand if you like. Otherwise the thing appears to be made of candyfloss. So the number of fives that were coming up which we couldn't fight that you see because these were decisions made in the privacy of the classroom and was really what the inspector said about what a class of children were doing with their teacher, about which there was no comeback. I can't escape the conspiratorial overtones about this you see. Somehow or other the inspector presented to the governing board right at the end of the week, the numbers of fives and so on, kept our over-arching percentages of satisfactory lessons in terms of progress and achievement and on the other categories, lower than was acceptable under the terms of personal failing or being in severe difficulties. And so the feeling of being stitched up was extremely strong at the time and still is, although we couldn't do anything about it. And the three teachers who were named to me to be failing, I just could not believe. It was difficult not to identify them because we were in almost all areas of the school single form entry, so if the report said that the teaching was unsatis-factory in year six, there was only one year six teacher so the thing becomes fairly clear. I would put my salary on the fact that the year six teacher and the year five teacher and the year two teacher were all at least average if not above. They'd done fantastic work to the delight and praise of our parent body over years and years. And yet here they are after four days labelled as being failed. This shocked my own feelings about my level of judgement to the core. Had I been wrong all these years? Or the governors? Or all the pupils who came through the system, or the secondary school accepting most of our chil-dren who provided hard evidence that our youngsters were making more progress at that school than children from other schools? What was the explanation as to why we were failed?

When Colin and his staff were accused by a LEA inspector of refusing to come to terms with the failure and they had all gone into a state of denial about it, Colin became extremely angry:

When one of the County inspectors said to me, 'Your teachers are in denial', I could have cheerfully punched him. Because what the teachers were saying was that the inspection team got it wrong; they failed us. We didn't fail the community. So we could say, 'We deny that we were doing a bad job'. I said, 'One person's denial was another person's refusal to accept untruths'.

Richard, who originally was confused about Ofsted's judgements, now did not believe the inspection was a 'done deal' before it ever started as some teachers did. He rationalised failure as follows:

And the rawness didn't go away for some people and so it was eventually too much. Many, many people did not want to accept that the findings of Ofsted were fair. They wanted to believe that for instance it was a hit squad. They wanted to believe that everything was hunky dory, that we'd been got at, we'd been shafted, there was a political agenda here, all this kind of bollocks. And I wasn't really interested in that at all. There were many, many things that Ofsted found – and they could have found many more if they'd actually spent more time here – which were wrong. And I'd known about for a long time but I couldn't really put my finger on it because even though I'd had experience of teaching before, even though I'd been in this school for four years, I always felt like a new boy, a beginner. There were people who'd been in teaching for twenty-five years, thirty years and I always assumed that they knew what they were talking about. But it became increasingly apparent to me that they didn't. They were like many many teachers up and down the country, up until the curriculum came along, they came to work, decided what they were going to do that morning, got into the classroom, shut the door and got on with it. And there was still that kind of very prevalent mentality among some teachers. That they – by virtue of the fact they'd done x number of years – they knew what they were talking about. But they didn't. They just didn't. I've seen some appalling things go on but who was I to speak. I was just a new boy on the block.

Transcending failure and shame

Rather than having one of their selves 'destroyed' (Goffman, 1952) by the experience of failure and shame, some of the teachers passed through what Anthony described as a 'cleansing' or 'healing' period. In this phase they regained confidence and a sense of self-worth. Colin said that some had found it necessary to 're-invent themselves to re-establish self-esteem'. Some teachers were 'girded' into action and saw special measures as a 'new starting point'. Richard was 'galvanised into action' and 'excited by all the changes that could be made'. Whereas he felt he was 'looking out for number one', Sean saw transcending failure and shame as a team effort:

> I think my confidence will come back hopefully as I work with a team who have the sort of courage of their own convictions and actually working things out for the good of the children over a period of time. And developing that confidence again in the fact that we're doing an okay job.

Recovery was marked by strong degrees of self-determination for some. Richard 'wouldn't let the bastards grind him down' and Joan said:

No, no. I wouldn't give in. I was determined, even if I stayed here till I was sixty-five, to get out of special measures. Because I felt I couldn't have left and got another job. Some people did. But I felt, for me, I had to stay and prove something.

For some, being in special measures had been a 'learning experience'. Vanessa gained promotion on the strength of it:

> JOAN: She got another job with an extra point and more responsibility. Being in special measures actually stood her in good stead that she'd had that experience. It didn't work against her, it worked for her. Because people thought well if she'd done all this. Because you're working at a faster pace than most people and you're having to get everything right, whereas people who pass Ofsted, maybe aren't involved in half the things that we're involved in because we're under such scrutiny. So I can look on the plus side.

Although Joan had been off sick for a term with depression she returned and came out of special measures 'strengthened' by the experience. She is now 'not scared of anything' and is seeking promotion in other schools.

Anthony, as a 'turning round' headteacher, had obviously gained a great deal professionally and personally from the experience though there are signs that his commitment is becoming rather more instrumental:

> I knew I was coming into a school in special measures. I wanted to do that because I'd turned a school round pre Ofsted days but when I got there they had 71 per cent level one or lower SATs results in reading and writing at KS 1 and nearly three quarters of their children were under-achieving. Now when I left six years on, KS 1 results were above national average and KS 2 results in Science and Maths were there and nearly there in English. So I wanted to use that to see if I could be more efficient and be better at it and be quicker at it. And I have been. That bit of it's given me a big buzz. I know I've moved on professionally, dealing with redundancies, dealing with moving a teacher on I was able to do in a way that was better for the school and better for that person and those people. And the quality of our SATs will rise and then the work that underpins that will slowly develop in quality and quantity. I know that we're going to be a success and I have no doubt about it at all. But the summer and autumn term were almost a bridge too far. I wouldn't have wanted one more term of it. Which was why we put so much energy into achieving it quickly. I wouldn't do it again. The personal cost is too much. I wasn't paid enough for it and there was no issue of being paid enough for it, of being paid more for it. I could run a nice school that still had work to do but would be a fraction of the stress and workload of the last two terms.

So if I'm one of those heads that they're looking for – people with experience of doing this who've all gone on and taken on those jobs. But I'd need a heck of a lot more money to do it again.

Headteachers can now gain a career boost by demonstrating on their curriculum vitae that they have turned schools round. Sean felt that this was the motivation behind the two temporary headteachers' secondments to Gladstone Street:

> We had two temporary heads who I felt were both here to prove a point, a personal point, because they were moving up the ladder and this was a sort of stepping stone – to be seen to be sorting out a failed school. So they had their own personal agendas. I felt they were trying to show the LEA how good they were in sorting staff out and showing teachers how to actually do it properly.

Goffman (1952) argues that one person's trouble is another's *Schadenfreude*. Sean felt this to be the case with the LEA inspectors who he felt 'had to be seen to make their mark with a failing school'. Thus, failure, shame and destruction of the self for some could be considered as career advancement for others.

Conclusion

Gladstone Street teachers are not alone in their experiences. Stoll and Myers (1998: 4), for example, state that 'in visits to such (i.e. 'failing') schools, we have heard harrowing stories of shock, desperation, hopelessness and helplessness, similar to the experiences of those facing bereavement'. They also acknowledge that policies of blame and shame, zero tolerance of failure and the 'sensationalist and hypercritical language used by politicians and the media' (Hargreaves, 1998a: 328):

> have contributed to low teacher morale and feelings of impotence, and through the drip feed of regular exposure to horror stories encouraged the public to believe that standards are low in the majority of schools, and that a significant minority is in a state of perpetual crisis.

Further, the policy of 'naming, blaming and shaming' rests on the view that schools can 'act independently of local socio-economic contexts' (Rea and Weiner, 1998: 21), and that school failure can be explained solely by reference to ineffectiveness in teaching and leadership (Slee et al., 1998). This is argued in spite of estimations by researchers influential in government circles that only 8–12 per cent of the difference in pupils' overall attainment is attributable to school effects (Reynolds et al., 1996); and in spite of the admission in a national policy document that

> there is certainly a link between socio-economic deprivation and the likelihood that a school will be found failing ... 7 per cent of schools with disadvantaged pupils have been found to be failing, compared to the national 'failure rate' of 1.5–2 per cent (DfEE and Ofsted, 1995: 12).
>
> (cited in Stoll and Myers, 1998: 11)

In fact, many of Gladstone Street's teachers argued that, in their view, the school, save for the improved SATs scores, was no better after leaving special measures than it was when entering. Indeed, in some respects, it could be considered worse. Half way through special measures a group of articulate middle class parents complained to Anthony about the school's increasing concentration on and pressure for increasing 'standards' in the children's academic work at the expense of other aspects of their education. This group explained at a school meeting that they had chosen the school for their children because of its multicultural ethos and curriculum. They were objecting to the decision to reduce time spent on celebrating and learning about customs and festivals in a wide range of cultures. This time was to be devoted to preparation for increasing pupil performance in the National Curriculum. Cultures of naming, blaming and shaming also have negative implications for 'successful' schools. As Fink argues, 'Effective schools which can be described as having professional learning communities can be reduced to mediocrity when nested in a larger culture of negativity and abuse' (Fink, 1999: 139). This can be even more the case if the responsibility for any perceived inadequacy is misdirected. Fink concludes that:

> The placing of blame on the school as the total explanation of failure is wrong-headed and self-defeating. Attempting to promote change by using shame, guilt or bully tactics will fail in the long run. While not only being ethically reprehensible, such tactics fail to account for context ... contextual factors like demographic shifts, government policies, inept local leadership, enrolment variations, inadequate succession planning for school leaders, among other factors, have more to do with school failure than the perceived inadequacies of teachers or heads.

Apart from this, such a policy creates a context that transforms teacher emotions from positive to negative, with potentially serious consequences for the education of their pupils. Teachers have to 'feel right' (Riseborough, 1981) in order to do their job to the best of their abilities. This is demonstrably not the case with regard to 'failing' schools.

3 Bullying in the workplace

The emotional politics of teacher stress

Introduction

The phenomenon of bullying is now widespread. One website devoted to
the topic of bullying in the workplace (Field, 2000) reveals that between
1 January 1996 and 5 February 1999, 3,498 enquiries were received with
2,886 cases of bullying being identified. Of these, 20 per cent were teachers,
lecturers or other school staff. A recent large-scale survey (Cooper and
Hoel, 2000) of 5,300 respondents drawn from seventy public and private
sector organisations reported 10.5 per cent of respondents stating that they
had been bullied at work. The authors argue that in real terms this suggests
that more than two million people at work consider themselves as being
bullied. And one in four people reported to have been bullied within the
last five years. Teaching was amongst those occupations with the highest
incidence of bullying. More than a third of the teachers surveyed said they
had been victimised by colleagues or managers in the past five years
(Thornton, 1999). Whitehead (1996: 6) claimed that 10,000 teachers experienced bullying at the hands of colleagues, and that it was the biggest
cause of stress-related illness in the profession. Headteachers in their forties
were the biggest perpetrators, followed by deputy headteachers and heads
of department. Victims were often the most experienced and strongest
personalities, with women in their mid-forties and primary school deputy
heads particularly at risk. Those who are currently bullied 'consistently
report the poorest health, the lowest work motivation and satisfaction, the
highest absenteeism figures and turnover intentions as well as the lowest
productivity, compared to those who were not bullied' (Cooper and Hoel,
2000: 2). The authors calculate that 'bullying may contribute to the loss
of as much as 18.9 million working days annually' (ibid.: 3)

Hitherto, bullying has tended to be seen in personal and psychological
terms, often being portrayed as the behaviour of psychotic individuals (for
example see Field, 1996). As Hargreaves (1998a: 318) argues, 'There have
been few socio-politically informed analyses that put a prime emphasis on
teacher emotions in the context of how teachers' work is organized and
how it is being reorganized through educational reform.' One exception

here is Reay (1996: 5), who argues that 'bullying cascades through the system so that some main grade teachers actually describe themselves as repositories for tensions working their way down through the educational system'. Teachers acting out their roles may not always realise what they are doing when they bully (see, for example, Woods et al., 1997: 160–1).

Blase and Anderson (1995: 40–1) draw attention to the connection with wider forces:

> Teacher emotions are professionally affected by the micro-politics of their schools in terms of their principal's behaviour, their experiences of change, and so on . . . these micro-politics of the school are in turn embedded within major macro-political forces of leadership, change and political reforms that have equally significant consequences for the emotions of teaching and teacher development.
>
> (Hargreaves, 1998a: 326–7)

In this chapter, we focus on the emotional politics of bullying in primary teaching. We draw on two definitions of bullying by trade unions that resonate well with the experiences and the meanings held by teachers in this research who claim that their bullying involved micro-political situations and the abuse of power. The ATL (1996: 1) defines bullying as 'The persistent (and normally deliberate) misuse of power or position to intimidate, humiliate or undermine.' In similar vein, the trade union Manufacturing, Science and Finance (MSF, 1994, cited at Field, 2000) defines it as: 'Persistent, offensive, abusive, intimidating or insulting behaviour, abuse of power or unfair penal sanctions which makes the recipient feel upset, threatened, humiliated or vulnerable, which undermines their self-confidence and which may cause them to suffer stress.' The two outstanding features in both are the misuse of power and the humiliation of individuals.

A majority of the teachers participating in the research reported having experienced bullying in this sense in the workplace. We explore the forms bullying took; the social, psychological and emotional impact it had on the teachers and, in Chapter 5, the coping strategies they used. We argue that the bullying phenomenon arises in the first instance with government policy and discourse. Policy makers see school managers as the means of implementing the reforms in the schools. Fulfilling these roles places managers under considerable pressures themselves. While managers are cast as the agents of change, they partly have to fulfil this role by changing themselves. Thus, in the new order, headteachers retain their traditional powers (in fact they have increased considerably), but delegate some duties and responsibilities to senior management teams and curriculum co-ordinators. Despite these changes, the purpose of management, it is argued, remains the same – to gain teachers' commitment to change and motivation for work, while exercising control over them (Friedman, 1977; Grace, 1995). Ball (1994) has argued that, despite rhetorics of autonomy and empowerment, new systems of management are a powerful and pervasive way of controlling teachers' work.

Headteachers' bullying strategies

The most commonly reported form of bullying of teachers was by their headteachers. Beatty (1999: 22) argues that 'teachers and their leaders are engaged in a powerful emotional relationship' and 'the various interactions and quality of relationships between headteachers and teachers colour the emotional practice of teaching' (ibid.: 29). Further, Blase and Anderson (1995) strongly emphasise the importance of the headteacher in shaping micro-political relationships in the school. Of all the forms of bullying reported to Cooper and Hoel (2000), 75 per cent of bullying cases involved managers bullying staff.

We will focus on the experiences of five teachers from the core sample. These were in mid- to late career and had a wide range of experience in schools (Mary, fifty-three years old; Jackie, fifty years old; Olivia, fifty-nine years old; William, forty-five years old; Jeremy, forty-two years old). All had held posts of responsibility. Mary, for example, had been a deputy headteacher of an infant school. All believed themselves to be 'victims' of bullying. Whereas, for some, bullying was the source of their stress and lengthy absence from work, for others, bullying commenced on their return to school following absence due to stress-related illness.

The teachers described to us the strategies their headteachers used to 'undermine' them personally and professionally. They were used by male and female headteachers equally, and were often used in concert, and repeatedly (the 'drip, drip effect' see Reay, 1996). As a consequence, the teachers felt *humiliated, tormented, disparaged* and *overloaded*.

Humiliated

Teachers were 'personally attacked and made to look small' (Olivia). Mary had been frequently verbally attacked in private and in public. This included being censured by the headteacher in front of her class. William was treated in this way over what seemed a relatively minor incident in a PE lesson. As he explained:

> I was out on the field taking a games lesson and some of the balls were flat. I said to a couple of children, 'Can you go back to the PE store and change them for some decent ones'. And they seemed to be gone for ages, so I just ran back round to the hut to say, 'Come on, hurry up with those balls, hurry up, we're all waiting'. When I came back, and it was only a couple of minutes or so, my class were all lined up

against the school wall with the headteacher there. And she said, 'You've left your children unattended'.

In addition to being 'told off' in front of the class he was given a written warning about future offences. He was so humiliated by this experience that he was too ashamed to tell his wife (a teacher) because she would 'explode' if she ever found out he had been treated like that.

Some teachers received public 'tellings off' in staff meetings. Jackie, having had a disagreement over the disciplining of children in the year group she was responsible for, was publicly demoted:

> Of course the more of a stand I made the more uncomfortable my life was and that was one of the reasons why he took the year co-ordinator's job off me. Because he and I weren't getting on at all well and actually he was encouraging the children to undermine me. I got very upset. Not so much because he did it but because of the manner in which he did it. I had a non-contact lesson just after lunch. And he caught me in the corridor. He said 'Oh, I'd like to speak to you at break time. Could I have a word with you. It won't take long'. And I said 'I'm on duty. So if you want to see me, what about my non-contact?' He said 'Oh yeah, that's fine. That's fine'. And I thought it was more about the disciplinary hearing because the governors were going to interview me about it. He kept saying, 'Do you want to retract'. And I said, 'No, I won't. I am perfectly clear in my mind that I've done the right thing'. It turned out to be nothing to do with the disciplinary hearing. He said, 'The chair of the governors and I have decided to take your responsibility post from you. We feel that you're getting stale and it's for the best and I'm going to announce it at the staff meeting tonight'. This was going to take place in about an hour and a half. So I had an hour and a half's warning that he was publicly going to announce that I was not going to be in that job any longer.

In another incident she, as chief editor of the school's magazine, had delayed its publication in order to carefully proof-read the work she had spent hours preparing. This annoyed the headteacher who had instructed the secretaries to duplicate it:

> He did actually come up to my class and shout at me in front of the children. I've never seen children look so shocked. . . . He was yelling and shouting, and his face was bright red and I just had to let him go on and go on. . . . I don't know why he got so upset about that, because I would have thought that as I'd been doing all the work I ought to see the final product before it was actually photocopied and sent out to four hundred children. And then he backed down and said, 'Oh,

I didn't realise that you hadn't seen it'. But by that time all the damage was done because I'd been humiliated again in front of my class. Even if he did back down, which he very rarely did, you still lose a lot of face don't you, when you've been made to look small in front of other colleagues or pupils? That was the atmosphere.

Tormented

Some of the teachers were placed in a state of psychological suspense which caused them to worry excessively. Mary experienced what she referred to as 'death by brown envelope'. These letters, which she learned to fear, contained criticisms of her personal and professional conduct. Although they were delivered in an apparently neutral, bureaucratic way, the affect on her was highly emotional:

> Once I had several letters throughout the school day. And really when I look back on them now some of them were quite minor things. But because you had such low self-esteem you felt that these were another nail in the coffin all the time. And on the day when I had the letter saying that she was going to put me under competency procedures, this was pushed in the pigeon hole. I opened it in full view of the rest of the staff in the staffroom. Not knowing what it was. You know, that is not good practice.

Jackie received a 'disciplinary' letter in her pigeon hole on the last day of term and spent the holiday worrying and 'going over and over' the criticisms it contained. Jackie and Olivia waited nine months with 'disciplinary procedures hanging over their heads' and being 'kept on tenterhooks waiting for a hearing' (Olivia). William was told by his headteacher that his alleged unprofessional behaviour recorded in the 'written warning' would remain on his record for two years but would be torn up after this time if there was no re-occurrence.

Disparaged

The teachers considered that their personal and professional selves were subjected to constant criticism. Some bullying headteachers did not acknowledge the achievements of their teachers. Mary said she had the 'head from hell' who 'never praises, always bullies' and felt that she was in a 'no win situation'. The headteacher found everything wrong with her – 'wrong size, wrong shape etc.'. William 'couldn't do right for doing wrong'. Olivia found herself the object of 'constant denigration' as the headteacher used to 'list a category of her "errors"'. Mary, who was being monitored as part of competency proceedings, found her headteacher to have a 'nit-picking attitude' and made 'nit-picking comments':

I found out that the head and so-called monitoring systems would mean, instead of focusing on the agreed issue, focus on minor things that had gone wrong or that she felt were an issue and that I didn't necessarily feel were an issue. For instance, there was something about pencils should be out on the children's tables. And she really laboured the point about the groups in the class and colour codes for the books and I had to keep the books out on a surface or in trays. She or the deputy head observed my lessons. She never actually said anything about the issues on which we were supposed to be concentrating. And because she homed in on these very minor points she was putting me into a position of even lower self-esteem because I was being attacked and vigorously attacked. Because she went on and on and on and on and on and on and on about them. And when I thought that I had given adequate replies to her question she still went on about it. But I understand this is typical of a bully that they do go on and on like that.

William, on returning to school following long-term sick leave with stress-related illness, had his absences closely monitored and felt 'censured' by the headteacher each time he was absent.

Overloaded

For all of these teachers the workload they had been undertaking had been a major contribution to their stress and subsequent illness. Mary described her headteacher as a 'martinet who pressured beyond the call of duty'. This headteacher had increased her demands that the teachers duplicate their planning documents at the time the government were 'backtracking' on the bureaucratic load for teachers. Some of the teachers received telephone calls and letters while ill at home that assumed that they could continue with such tasks as curriculum planning and report writing. Jeremy said that the headteacher and governors 'were interested in the work getting done but just didn't care about my health'. These teachers found that their headteachers could control their work by manipulating its volume, pace and resourcing, resulting in further overload. The teachers had found an increase in 'pressure' on returning to work after stress-related illness. Jackie, who had been promised a 'staged' return to work, found herself with a full workload plus the increased commitments of, for example, playground duty, parents' evenings and co-ordinator's meetings. Control of resource allocation also enabled the headteachers to deprive some of the teachers of support staff thus increasing their workload. For example, Jackie was not given any learning support teacher time to work with the SEN children in a particularly 'difficult' class. Her school was experiencing very serious disciplinary problems and the school's non-replacement of the deputy headteacher resulted in children being sent to her as year leader for disciplinary reasons, disrupting her lessons and adding considerably to her workload.

William's school had a successful inspection and he and the other teachers thought they would be able to 'rest on their laurels' for a few months afterwards as they had put so much effort into the inspection. However, he found the pace and volume of work did not decrease – rather the opposite. Working in a school where the headteacher wanted 'constant improvement' meant having 'hidden cameras watching us all the time' and being under 'constant surveillance and monitoring':

> We're having lessons watched twice a week at the moment, you can't relax, it's constant pressure. When you know you're going to be watched you think, 'I will put a bit more oomph into this lesson'. But nobody can do wowee lessons every lesson of the day, every day of the week. It just isn't possible. People aren't living in the real world. It's that feeling that you've got to be doing wonderful things all the time.

This headteacher also had other high expectations of the teachers' work rates:

> WILLIAM: This letter came round a couple of times asking what clubs we were going to run. And I decided I wasn't going to run any and signed it and sent it back. It would arrive on my desk again in a couple of days and I would just sign and return it. That hasn't gone down very well at all.

The headteacher's presence at school was highly visible and attested to her personal commitment to and capacity for work.

> WILLIAM: If I drive past in the evening she's there at seven o'clock. If I go past on a Saturday morning on my way into town, her car's there. And I just wonder how much longer she can sort of keep it going – whether she'll burn herself out.

William felt her visibility further underlined the work expectations she held for the staff – if she was there, then so should they be.

The impact of bullying on the teacher's self

Hargreaves (1998a: 323) argues that 'Teachers' emotions are rooted in and affect their selves, identities and relationships with others'. Beatty (1999: 20) has illustrated this, finding that, in her research, 'negative experiences with principals affected the self of some teachers; they were often associated with long standing hurt, resentment, alienation and loss of personal and professional confidence'. Similarly among our sample, bullying had an emotional impact on the teacher's self.

All our teachers, up to the point where they were stressed and ill, had been developing their careers. All had previously coped with major life events (Pearlin, 1989), including severe illness, divorce, bereavement, supporting severely disabled children or parents. Mary felt she was a 'strong person'. Jeremy had previously 'always gone into work – even when I was ill'. They all stated that they considered that they were not the type of people who suffer illness from stress. Jackie said:

> My doctor was aware that this situation was happening to lots of other people and being quite angry at seeing what was happening to me. Because he'd seen me through lots of illnesses and he saw me through thyroid cancer and he saw me battle back and get back to work and work my way in to having a bit of a career again.

All the teachers in this group, did not, at the onset of their illness, realise fully what was happening to them. Jeremy felt 'blurred and couldn't concentrate'. William 'couldn't believe what was happening'. Jeremy likened the feeling to the ending of a film in which the last words uttered by Steve McQueen were 'What the hell went wrong?' Jeremy's wife sat him down and told him he was ill. This new state was a departure from the 'normality' of the past:

> OLIVIA: I'm still on anti-depressants. I've never taken anything like that in my life before. Not even in the two years when I was being tested by the children in my probationary year.

Illness manifested itself in a number of physical, psychological and emotional ways. The men experienced physical collapse. All the teachers 'broke down' in the GP's surgery. The somatic symptoms reported included: suspected angina; suspected ulcers; high blood pressure; being observed for a coronary condition; sleeplessness; diverticulosis; irritable bowel syndrome; skin conditions; and physical, mental and emotional exhaustion. All were diagnosed as having depression and received both medication and psychodynamic counselling; one undertook cognitive therapy. Jeremy contemplated suicide but was counselled by his GP.

All the teachers had negative feelings about themselves. Olivia, who had complained about her headteacher stealing money, worried because she didn't want to be seen as a disloyal 'crap teacher who had shopped the head' and her 'self-confidence evaporated'. Jackie had a 'grey cloud over' her, her 'self-esteem had gone' and she felt 'worthless'. Mary was 'rendered impotent' and her 'self-esteem undermined'. Jackie felt guilt and her sense of efficacy was damaged:

> It's very difficult to explain how low you get. You just feel that you're really worthless people. You feel you've been conning people all these years and that you've never actually been able to do the job at all.

William felt that however much he did 'it wasn't enough'. All considered they were unique in feeling the way they did. However, after receiving support and knowledge from friends and colleagues (see Chapter 5), they began to interpret their experiences as bullying by management. Olivia said:

> Once I'd picked myself up and was getting better, once I'd realised all my friends were people who have a care for me, I began to realise that perhaps it wasn't me. Perhaps it was her (headteacher). And the feeling of anger that I have has strengthened in the past twelve months. It hasn't diminished. And that, I think, again indicates that it was her that was wrong and not me. Do you see what I mean? That the emotional reaction is still very strong. And apart from that I've now come across several other people, who I think are still at the beginning, who have been knocked around worse than I have by the County Council and are taking legal action. Personal injury claims. And that again made me realise that up until July of last year (July 1997), I thought perhaps I was the only person – the only teacher in the County who was being singled out as a crap teacher.

At first they felt 'numbness and anger' (Jackie), 'embittered' (William), 'outraged at the injustice' (Jeremy), 'insulted', 'victimised', 'don't deserve this, it's very unfair' (William), 'hatred' (Mary). Olivia felt guilty, blamed herself for what had happened and wanted to 'find ways to put things right'. However, at the same time, she experienced strong feelings of anger and asked 'how dare they make me ill?' Jeremy, who had previously had 'great difficulty keeping his emotions down', developed very aggressive behaviour towards others and would 'punish iron' by training aggressively on weight lifting machines at the gym.

Blase and Anderson (1995: 8) note how 'violations of fair and equitable treatment have been linked to decreases in teacher morale'. Jeremy felt his school management had destroyed his enthusiasm and trust which were both essential in his teaching:

> Teachers demand of themselves things which management don't really understand. And I think that's a confidence which management has to have in teachers and the autonomy that they have. Although it's being eroded, it is very real to them. They get the buzz from the job and if you lose that it's like having fluid drawn out of you like a spider draws fluid out of a fly. You're left like a husk. The problems and the crises were engendered by the new management's tactics. They compounded the problem. And the bullying factor is not lost on me. I would not be very happy with going back into a room with somebody in a senior management position. I don't think I'd be prepared to trust anybody. I'd think that there was another agenda. And I'm not paranoid – I'm hyper-vigilant, I think is the word I'd use. I keep re-checking reality. Trust and confidence have been breached. Without

a doubt. And it's provable. I think we've reached that stage. If that cancer gets into a school and it's not made public and it's not made known, there's a problem. Cancers can happen in a month, they can happen in six months, they can happen in a year. That style of management cannot be condoned.

The teachers' perceptions of the purpose of bullying

Removal

All the teachers believed that the basic motive behind the headteacher's behaviour was to remove them from their jobs. This can be seen as a product of restructuring. In the light of government reforms, teachers needed to change, and pressure was brought to bear accordingly. Those who were reluctant or unable to change should be removed. This was a very traumatic experience as the teachers had obviously invested much in career terms. Mary said, 'I've given my life to teaching – my career was a priority.' And Jeremy argued that 'Your credibility, your career, your esteem and standing. These things are nurtured over many years.' Olivia believed, 'The headteacher wants me out.' Jeremy was offered redundancy, it was put to him by the headteacher to sound like an offer of some 'alternative career opportunity rather than the sack'. Jackie explained that her head-teacher had

> gradually whittled down the numbers of people that stood up to him. He did it in different ways. But the staff turnover was quite tremendous. If you look at the number of people who have left in the last two or three years, it's an awful lot. Something was basically wrong in the school.

Mary thought the headteacher 'wanted rid of dead wood' and to 'bring in her own people'. She felt 'they wanted me out and I didn't have any fight left'. Mary had returned from eight months' sick leave to face competency procedures (see Chapter 1), which management used as 'a stick to beat her with', and she felt 'it didn't matter what I did, they weren't ever going to pass me'. William, who had also returned following a lengthy absence, was taking days off for recurring illness, for example a perforated eardrum, but also, on one occasion, took a morning off to look after his sick children. He had a morning's pay 'docked' by the headteacher although other teachers doing the same thing were not penalised. His absences were now carefully monitored and he said that in future he would telephone the school to say he had a migraine rather than looking after his children. He felt the headteacher was going to use the evidence of absence and his other 'unprofessional behaviour' to eventually remove him from his post.

The teachers were also quite clear about their headteacher's reasons for wanting them removed. Jackie thought age was a major factor:

> I think the job has changed. One of the things that would have made it possible to keep going on till you're older was the fact that because you were older and had more experience you had a bit more status. But I don't think that seems to be the case at the moment. They seem to value young, energetic people straight from college with lots of ideas. That seems to be the thing that certainly the governors look to – people who have got no family commitments and people who want to spend more time doing clubs. But if you've got a family you can't just spend hours and hours zooming off here, there and everywhere all the time. I have to take clubs and a range of things. It's difficult isn't it? Because you've got the advantage of being more mature and seen life and have brought your own children up, but that doesn't seem to have as much weight as being cheap and having more free time. I think older teachers are demoralised. They've been through so many changes and have been expected to accept so many different philosophies and teaching methods. Generally they're not looked up to are they?

William thought ideological reasons were as important as youth, lack of commitments and finances:

> Most schools are in financial difficulties and are going for NQTs. Experience actually works against you now. Experience doesn't count for anything. It just means you're expensive and have an opinion about things. Most schools will appoint somebody much younger who they can mould in their own image. They're always wanting more from everybody. No matter what you do they'll always want more. It's not just teaching is it? What you've done in the past doesn't count for anything. It's what you're going to do in the future that counts. And if you're not going to spend all your life working at school then I think some schools are not going to be interested in taking you on.

Being a teacher now increasingly involves work that lies beyond the classroom (Campbell and Neill, 1994). It takes the forms of planning, administration, and supervision of colleagues' work and of involvement in the external relations of marketing and work in and with the community. As workloads increase, teachers experience intensification, which erodes time for reflection and leisure (Apple, 1986; Hargreaves, 1994). With this have come new conceptions of what 'good teaching' constitutes.

While extra-curricular activities were theoretically voluntary for the teachers at William's school, there were clearly very strong expectations from the headteacher that teachers would organise them. William perceived she was prioritising this aspect largely for marketing purposes. He had a long history of running games clubs at the school but had 'downshifted' (see Chapter 4) some of his responsibilities and felt resentment at being asked to do this extra work after experiencing bullying: 'I feel like saying, "Sod it, why the hell should I? Why should I give up my time?"' He thought that bullying 'was not the way to get the best out of people if you're constantly nagging at them all the time', and it had profoundly affected his commitment and loyalty:

> If she expects me to be loyal then I'm not going to be anymore. This is what I feel. I don't feel very inspired to do any more.

Like Beatty's (1999: 16) teachers these examples serve to show that:

> The alienation and marginalisation of dissenters, as a means of control and maintenance of the status quo, was evidently emotionally costly for these teachers and for their students and their schools as they became disengaged and withdrawn from their work.

Personal deficiencies of headteachers

Even if restructuring, new teacher roles and a new career structure (see Chapter 4) and headteachers' micro-political manoeuverings were major factors behind the escalation of bullying, there were also seen to be personal shortcomings on the part of headteachers. In other words, bullying – together with its effects – is not an inevitable consequence of restructuring. Our teachers referred to two such shortcomings – inadequacy and indiscretion.

Inadequacy

Olivia felt that her female headteacher had 'projected her inadequacies' onto her. The headteacher had:

> fallen into this job just because she was in the right place at the right time. And in those days it was easy. She'd not been carrying on any role or had the experience of organising all the things that a head-teacher has to do. And I think psychologically her approach was always aggressive. But it didn't show until she was then under pressure. It's cascade governing isn't it, from the government down. Because teachers and schools are under pressure to implement all these changes in order to move up standards. She sort of cascaded it down to me.

Here, Olivia echoes Reay's (1996) point earlier alluding to a more general inadequacy among managers at the mercy of the new system. But there were more individual inadequacies. Jackie described her headteacher as inadequate and with a 'chip on his shoulder'. Sometimes headteachers were seen to lack expertise in particular aspects of education. Mary said her female headteacher 'didn't know anything about infants'. Some lacked experience and were considered to have been promoted too soon (William's headteacher was in her early thirties) or had managed to gain promotion at a time before the demands of the headteacher's role had begun to intensify (Grace, 1995: Woods et al., 1997). Jackie described her headteacher as 'good at mismanagement rather than management'. Mary described her headteacher as 'not a people person' and William's lacked interpersonal skills and 'rubbed people up the wrong way, lacked sympathy and was rude':

> She's not got a very good manner with people. Certainly if you don't agree with something, she tends to get pretty cross, pretty quickly about it. It's really very difficult to have a discussion about things. You tend to get rather put in your place really.

Jackie's headteacher lacked the interpersonal skills needed to unite the staff of an amalgamated school. Schools reorganised in this way are notoriously stressful and difficult to both manage and work in (Dunham, 1984; Draper, 1993). Mary felt that her headteacher had 'ridden roughshod over the feelings of the staff'. William considered his headteacher to be a 'hard woman manager' who had no family and therefore lacked understanding of his domestic situation and child care problems:

> She's married, newly married, no children. And I did say I felt I was being penalised for having children really. I now take my own children to school and before I used to be at school much earlier, now it's about twenty five past eight. Much later than I've ever been before. But there is that sort of, 'Well you weren't here at quarter past eight when I came along to your room to see you'. It's the sort of way that it's put really. Or she will say, 'You'd gone home when I wanted to speak to you' about something. I hope she gets pregnant actually. If she had children of her own it might soften her up a bit. I just feel – it's a very sexist thing to say about a woman – but her outlook might change a bit.

Some headteachers were seen as unprofessional because of their 'irrational' behaviour. These headteachers 'constantly changed the goal posts' and 'you didn't know what you were supposed to be doing from one day to the next' (Olivia). Jackie said her headteacher, 'changed his management style every new moon' (see Chapter 1). Mary likened it to 'playing chess with the *Red Queen*'.

In some cases headteachers were seen to be indiscreet or dishonest, and the teachers felt a strong sense of injustice at this and the way they were being treated. Like Beatty's (1999: 25) teachers, our participants 'wanted a workplace which was a fair and just place'.

Indiscretion

Some of the headteachers were seen as 'totally unprofessional' and 'misrepresented' staff (Olivia). Others 'never told you to your face what you were doing wrong but went behind your back to tell others' (Jeremy). This headteacher had forged a development plan for the subject for which Jeremy was responsible. Some headteachers were thought to have stolen money or 'fiddled travelling expenses' (Olivia). Others used 'hidden rules' or invented 'spurious disciplinary procedures' for controlling teachers. Some made what were judged by the teachers to be false accusations against them. Jackie's headteacher withheld a day's pay from one of her colleagues who was experiencing personal difficulties:

> Because of having had to donate a kidney to her daughter she'd been treated very shabbily I thought. And in fact it was trying to support her that really started the unpleasantness. I just felt that somebody who's had to give a kidney to keep their daughter alive had quite a lot of trauma in the build-up to that, and she certainly needed as much support as she could get. And there were one or two things that he'd done to her. She had a day's pay docked when I'd advised her to go home – because apparently the secretary hadn't been told the following morning. And the head said, 'Oh well, I was in a bad mood'. And he never actually did give her the money back. He just gave her a day off and then made us cover for her ... we were treated badly. It didn't matter that we had any lives.

In one school, the headteacher had 'favourites' in the Senior Management Team, this alienated the rest of the staff and if any of the senior managers 'fell out' with the headteacher they were 'cast into outer darkness' (Jackie). Sikes et al. (1985) argue that headteachers use promotions in order to develop 'latent status hierarchies' to support their own status orientations.

Conclusion

It might be claimed that the five teachers featuring in this chapter deserved the treatment they received. Perhaps they were not fit to teach and had resisted all attempts to enskill them. They might have been doing children harm, and holding back the rest of the school from raising standards. However, the majority of the teachers participating in the research have considerable experience and records of being extremely able teachers. This is attested to by their LEAs, and many of them have been praised by Ofsted for the work they were doing. Mary had gained a deputy headship of an infant school after teaching for twenty-five years. Jeremy, as a curriculum co-ordinator, had contributed to his own professional development, and that of others, by carrying out classroom based research in curriculum development in humanities teaching. He disseminated his research in inservice training sessions at school and at a local polytechnic with students in initial teacher education and practising teachers taking advanced courses. He had developed his subject throughout his own school and had used his expertise on secondment as an advisory teacher for two years working in his LEA to introduce the National Curriculum. Jeremy successfully undertook training as an Ofsted inspector and carried out one inspection while still employed at his school. He considered the head-teacher's 'jealousy' of this role contributed to his bullying.

The views in this chapter, of course, are those of the teachers, and, as such, not an objective judgement on their headteachers. Nonetheless, they are a strong indication of breakdowns in relationships, the strength of which was such a notable feature of successful primary schools in the 1970s and 1980s. The culture of care and collaboration noted by such as Nias et al. (1989) and Acker (1999) has been replaced by one of fear and humilia-tion. The culture of care was marked by its emotional bonds among teachers in collaborative communities, as well as between teachers and pupils (Nias et al., 1992); the culture of fear is emotionally divisive. As in cultures of care, emotions are used in the new cultures to advance the values that underpin them. They arise through the exercise of power and control in arousing certain negative emotions. The resultant stress among some teachers has a meaning, a functionality, in spite of its emotional messiness.

In fact, the emotions expressed here bear remarkable similarity to those experienced by teachers during an Ofsted inspection as reported in Jeffrey and Woods (1998). There it was noted that teachers experienced professional uncertainty through confusion, anxiety, a sense of inadequacy, and the loss of positive emotions such as humour; also personal diminishment through mor-tification, dehumanisation, loss of their pedagogic values, and persecutory guilt. It was argued there that arousing these emotions, negative from the teachers' point of view, could be seen as in fact positive from the point of view of the restructuring reforms and of the agencies and management concerned with overseeing their implementation. The new educational world is domi-nated by the philosophy of economic rationalism. Emotions have little place here, indeed they can be an embarrassment. The Plowden Report (CACE, 1967) with its emphasis on care and child-centredness has been strongly cas-tigated in official circles. 'Too much caring, not enough learning' (Woods and Jeffrey, 1996: 55) was an early slogan of the new era. Teachers thus have to be purged of these feelings if they are to be reincorporated into their new roles. There is a new brand of professionalism here, which involves being part of a hierarchical management structure, less democratic participation, less auton-omy, more prescription. The trauma thus is functional in terms of the system, a rite of passage through which teachers proceed to the new state, varying in intensity according to teachers' levels of resistance or ability otherwise to adapt. Failure to adapt brings increased pressures that can now carry a sec-ondary function – removal – as noted in this chapter.

Even if we were to accept this argument, however, it would appear that the headteachers' personal qualities have had a great deal to do with the problems recounted here. There is abuse of power, which begins, arguably, with government policy in initiating the pressures on schools and the agencies and structures to enforce them. Even so, this 'abuse' is indirect, and there are institutional and individual factors, most notably in the person of the headteacher, that carry these pressures through to the point of stress and burnout for members of their staff. These are indeed clumsy attempts to make the system work. Headteachers, as gatekeepers, are usually skilled at filtering policy, at exploiting the 'implementation gap' between policy making and policy implementation (Ball and Bowe, 1992), at protecting their staff in the interests of their schools. There is little evidence of that here. It is the headteachers who are abusing their power. They do not have to act in this way.

However we interpret the headteachers' actions here, they are likely to be educationally counter-productive. They undermine teachers' self-confidence, cause identity crises, and generate a great deal of anger, grief and stress, which cannot fail to have a consequence for their pupils. Even more worrying is the escalation of bullying – a long-standing and deep-seated activity amongst pupils to everybody's great concern – to the staff of schools, the most important role models on offer to pupils. As we have seen, the behaviour is not hidden from them, but very much on display. It would appear important, in fact, that on occasions the pupils witness, and thus intensify, the bullying. What lesson are they learning here? Are these the kinds of relationships that we wish to encourage amongst them? Can we hope to deal with bullying among pupils while encouraging it amongst ourselves? This is behaviour more suited to schools of the nineteenth rather than to those of the twenty-first century.

4 Careers under stress

Teacher adaptations at a time of intensive reform

Introduction: teacher careers

The time is ripe for a reconsideration of teacher careers. Evetts (1987) argues that some studies of teacher careers assume a continuous and progressive trajectory. This model, it is argued, is founded on the concept of an 'objective' occupational career which is an ordered sequence of development extending over a period of years and involving steadily more responsible roles within an occupation. In teaching there are fewer and fewer opportunities for promotion as one ascends the scale, and the model is a kind of 'flattened pyramid' (Woods et al., 1997). Ethnographers, by contrast, have explored teachers' 'subjective' experiences of career (Sikes et al., 1985; Ball and Goodson, 1985; Cherniss, 1995). Here the 'emphasis is on the individual's construction of meaning and the career as a continuous process in which the individual changes in accordance with their own choices, aims and intentions' (Woods, 1983: 153). Individuals 'negotiate and re-negotiate in their own minds as their careers proceed and they continually set and reset the goals themselves in that process' (ibid.). Work carried out in this tradition has shown the centrality of the teachers' selves in this process and how their values and commitments shape their careers (Woods, 1981; Nias, 1980, 1995).

Feminist inspired work has challenged what it sees as the male-centred concept of 'objective career' by showing how the careers of the women teachers studied are 'discontinuous', 'broken' or 'interrupted' owing to child-rearing and other family commitments (Evetts, 1987). Acker (1992), for instance, shows in her analysis of women teachers that female careers in teaching are influenced by 'daily experiences in a workplace context'. Whereas males are often seen as 'rational career planners, busily plotting career maps and climbing career ladders', in contrast, women's 'career plans are provisional and changeable', influenced by 'family stage and the work needs of teachers' spouses, as well as unexpected life events' (ibid.: 148–9).

Career theorists have recognised that the steps and paths in careers are sometimes not very definite, and some careers end badly (Strauss, 1971). Maclean (1992) and Maclean and McKenzie (1991) seem to presuppose an exit from the occupation at retirement age, though briefly touch on the issues of 'dissatisfied leavers' and 'wastage' to the profession. Huberman (1993) discovered a professional trajectory in the professional life cycle that sometimes terminated in 'reassessment' leading to 'bitter disengagement' from teaching. Some reasons for leaving the career before retirement age were 'fatigue', 'routine', 'frustration', and 'nervous tension'. With this exception, however, career researchers/theorists have not given much attention to teachers' experience of early exit or the adaptations of those who change course in their teacher careers. An opportunity to investigate this phenomenon has been afforded by recent developments in teaching which have caused increasing levels of stress and brought the whole profession into crisis.

Teacher stress and supply

We argued in the introduction to this book that teacher stress is linked to the growing numbers of premature retirements, redundancies and re-deployments – the crisis in retention (Woods et al., 1997). We also argue that it is contributing to the increasing problems in teacher recruitment. These crises are particularly acute in London where many 'Commonwealth' (Australia, New Zealand, Canada) supply teachers, not trained in the National Curriculum, are employed (Menter et al., 1999). Relf and Hobbs (1999) argue that there is a downward spiral of low recruitment leading to low standards leading to low recruitment (see also Sutherland, 1997; Young, 1997). Many job vacancies remain unfilled (Howson, 1998, 1999). This situation is particularly acute for headteacher and senior manager posts in London schools (Menter et al., 1999). Such jobs have become 'blocked off' from teachers who formerly would have applied for them. The pressures of the headteacher role have become too great and the salary levels not high enough to compensate for them (Woods et al., 1997). The career structure base has become even wider in consequence. Thomson (reported in Slater, 2000: 30) found that, 'in 1998, over 3,000 teachers in England and Wales left the profession for other employment – half of them for work outside teaching. In 1993 the figure was just 2,000.' There are 'now as many people leaving education for other work as there are retiring at normal age or leaving to start a family'.

In an attempt to boost recruitment, the government has launched the national advertising campaign 'No-one Forgets a Good Teacher' (Booth in MacLeod, 1998) and has published a Green Paper (DfEE, 1998b) aimed at 'modernising' teaching, introducing what it views as a more attractive (performance related) pay structure in order to attract recruits to teaching. However, Dainton (1999: 45) argues that:

> 50 per cent of the teaching workforce is over forty-five years old. Yet proposals in the Green Paper have little to offer this important group

of teachers who help form the backbone of the profession. What are the prospects for an ageing, demoralised and disaffected workforce, already working under considerable stress and carrying a heavy workload, which saw the last government's arrangements as blocking off the only career prospects which had kept many going?

These developments have had radical implications for teacher careers. We draw on our study of teacher stress to investigate the consequences of stress for teacher careers, and teachers' own strategies and adaptations in adjusting their careers.

Changing views of careers

How did the teachers perceive what was happening to them in career terms? Their comments led us to the view that periods of teacher stress can be considered as 'epiphanies' (Denzin in Richardson, 1994) or 'fateful moments' (Giddens, 1991: 112) in the career:

> when individuals are called on to take decisions that are particularly consequential for their ambitions, or more generally for their future lives. Fateful moments are highly consequential for a person's identity.

They are likely to occur during 'periods of strain' and, like 'critical incidents' (Sikes et al., 1985: 57), are 'key events in an individual's life, around which pivotal decisions revolve. They provoke the individual into selecting particular kinds of actions which lead in particular directions,' and in which 'new aspects of the self are brought into being' (Becker, 1966: xiv). During episodes of stress, individuals may experience 'fateful moments' or 'critical incidents', in which processes of 'rumination' (Lazarus, 1990), 'reassessment' (Huberman, 1993) and 'redefinition' (Sikes et al., 1985) of self and career takes place. A succession of such moments during a period of stress has the potential for bringing about conditions where the individual takes a different career direction or terminates the career. In this process the individual 'chooses' a way and 'makes a self' (ibid.: 57).

Convery (1999) argues that such 'critical incidents' are commonly deployed by researchers to illustrate teachers' professional and personal development. In these cases the transformative nature of the incidents is used to suggest 'progressive moral improvement'. However, in the teachers' experience, the stress-related illness episodes were, like their subsequent thoughts of leaving teaching or having to modify their roles, wholly unanticipated and usually not at all transformative in a positive sense. The result was more like Goffman's (1968) 'spoiled careers', in that they were 'untimely terminated, or have otherwise taken a turn out of line with the occupants' intentions' (Woods, 1983: 63; see also Riseborough, 1981). A common phrase used by the teachers in the stress research was, 'I was the last person

I thought it (stress) would happen to.' The occupational changes they experienced as a consequence of their adaptations were in many cases out of their control. Some felt 'forced out' of teaching while others were 'trapped within' it (Woods et al., 1997).

Those teachers who had extended absence reported that they had thoughts of leaving teaching during their time off work with stress-related illness, yet the negative financial consequences of doing so loomed large. As in Becker's (1977) conception of career, these teachers had 'side-bets' and were, at this stage, committed *by* their work as much as *to* it. Those who had partners said that they had extensive discussions during their illness deciding whether they could afford not to return to work in teaching. This process, while a form of 'strategic life planning' (Giddens, 1991), was heavily constrained by such factors as age, gender, experience, the state of the labour market and the marketisation of schooling. Judith (forty-three years) was effectively facing career curtailment:

> I was very scared, let down I think. I didn't feel the headteacher had supported me – well any of us, I mean not just me, because everybody was feeling scared about it . . . I was anxious because I obviously had to pay the mortgage. And I was really worried that I couldn't get another job because I was expensive. Although I'd only been teaching for six years I think that would probably have taken me up to the top of the grade anyway, but because I was an adult – a mature student – I'd been given enhanced points when I started so I was right at the top of the scale, so I was expensive. So every job I applied for they were all saying, 'Newly qualified teachers welcome to apply'. So I thought, 'Well that's code for we don't want anybody who's expensive basically'. Also I wanted to look for a permanent contract and they were all of them temporary – one term, two terms, that kind of thing. I knew that I would have some redundancy payment, that was in the letter, it was all laid down. So I was determined not to take just a one-term contract. Because I knew I could cope with one or two terms, that wouldn't have been too difficult. But I didn't really want to have a break if I could avoid it.

Michael (fifty-two years) considered that he had been 'bullied' in the workplace and felt that his career was in the hands of the management who had been bullying him. On his return to school after extended sick leave he found management's behaviour towards him increased his stress and further confused his thinking about his career, and decisions concerning it seemed out of his control:

> I was still fatigued and finding it a struggle – the stress was continuing. They were keeping me on tenterhooks all the time. Nothing resolved, no issue clarified, no review of my job description, no clear-cut pointers

about my future. Would I still be a co-ordinator? If not, where did that leave me?' I was a relatively highly paid older member of staff ripe for being made redundant. They hadn't said, 'We've got to have two redundancies, can we have volunteers?' but there was this implication …

The experience of stress had changed the way all the teachers viewed their careers. While some (men and women) had held notions of the 'objective' career with its predictable stages (onwards and upwards) now, following stressful episodes, they were more focused on merely coping. Many of the teachers (particularly in mid-career) wondered if they could keep going until they were sixty years of age. For Jackie (fifty years) this involved the loss of ambition:

> But I do think my career reached its limit. I'm not going to go anywhere now. I think that's it. I've got no ambition left in me any more. I was actually going for deputy headships and jobs like that but I'm not any longer. I was getting interviews but I just don't care any more. I'm not interested in career other than doing what I'm doing now. I'm interested in teaching. I like teaching the way I am at the moment. And I'm not particularly interested in management any more. I think I've had so much of the stuffing knocked out of me I just haven't got enough energy left. I just don't want to be bothered. So although it might have made me more capable of resisting bullying or pressure it dampened down any ambition; it's just dampened it down completely.

Teacher adaptations

Given these changing views, how did our teachers adapt? Some of the teachers were determined to stay in teaching in some form and would not consider the early retirement or breakdown pensions they were offered; saying they would not 'let the system beat' them. Most of the teachers argued that the work they were expected to do was not the job they had trained for or entered teaching to do. For all of the teachers, no matter what age or career stage, stress meant a shift in their values from purely expressive to more instrumental commitment, a pattern that others have observed in primary teachers since the ERA of 1988 (Broadfoot and Osborn, 1988; Pollard et al., 1994; Jeffrey and Woods, 1996). In these circumstances what for some teachers had once been a vocation now became just a job. Apart from this, however, they chose three different kinds of adaptation: *retreatism*; *downshifting*; and *self-actualising*.

Retreatism

Woods (1995b: 9) argues that retreatism involves, 'submitting to the imposed changes in professional ideology leading to stress and anxiety. This can be alleviated in a number of ways, including leaving the job'. Pollard et al. (1994) found 'considerable evidence' of retreatism in response to the introduction of the National Curriculum and attendant intensification of work. This adaptation was particularly pronounced among the older teachers and at the time they were interviewed, the authors report, they were 'about to take early retirement or were strongly considering it' (ibid.: 101). Up till recently, internal retreatism, involving withdrawal to the classroom and working in isolation, was one form of 'escape' for teachers that might have been possible. However, this is no longer a viable adaptation given the levels of monitoring and surveillance and the ethos in schools today of constant improvement in a culture of managerial teamwork.

The teachers in the stress research who adapted in this way had gained or were seeking a breakdown pension considerably before the 'official' retirement age. They had no plans to return to teaching. Indeed, as part of the settlement for this form of early retirement it is against the regulations to return to teaching in any form as the individual has been deemed to be physically and psychologically unfit for teaching work. All the teachers in this category felt 'forced out' of teaching.

Marion (fifty years), for example, was very committed to child-centred teaching in an inner city context, and experienced stress with her over-conscientious approach to nurturing individual children (Campbell and Neill, 1994). Others have noted the association of guilt with burnout (Hargreaves, 1994). Marion grieved for a lost self (Nias, 1991) when she had to leave teaching with a breakdown pension because of her depressive illness. She had a very strong conception of 'normality' and 'abnormality' in work and felt that her career had finished 'abnormally'. Interestingly, for Marion, 'normal' life refers to working life at school and 'abnormal' refers to a life where you can 'visit galleries', 'go out for lunch' (things she has done since being retired). Retirement was, therefore, seen as an 'abnormal' state. Also, she had a conception of a 'normal' career with a 'normal' end to it, presumably with an appropriate rite of passage (party and presentation at school, letter from the CEO, a clock). Marion's end of career was 'abnormal' and undesirable, termination taking the form of a disabling illness caused by stress and burnout. Her friends said 'you can't leave like this', and she said 'I didn't want it to end this way, there is still a great sadness'. To her, her career was unfinished and incomplete.

Ben (thirty-eight years), who was very young to be considering retirement, could not envisage continuing in the job 'that has made me so ill'. He said that returning to a reduced role would be unthinkable for this reason, and he would feel that he had 'cheated' the school by not fulfilling the role for which he had been appointed:

> I don't think I'm going to be able to cope with teaching any more, with the way the system is and the pressures of the job. No. I think I've had enough of that. The job is a very stressful one and having

experienced what I've experienced since April there's no way I want to put myself in a situation where I can be made ill again. It's taken much longer than I anticipated to start getting well. The doctor said to me yesterday, 'It could take two or three years before you really feel a 100 per cent'. And I think he's right. I couldn't cope with it now. If I could find a job that was sufficiently lucrative without the pressure, I would get out of education. And I'm not bothered. I'll just see what happens. I look in the jobs section in the newspaper, more to give me an idea of what I might like to do. If I can manage, I'll work part-time to begin with. I think what I want to do is just get a pretty mundane job to begin with and just settle back into work and then take it from there. I have no desire to start a new career as such. I don't want a career. I don't want to go into something where there are prospects of management and moving up. I've been there and I've done it. I could just cope with working in a shop, something like that with very little responsibility. I'm no longer planning; just taking one day at a time.

Julie (thirty-five years) re-defined her role outside teaching. She left following her school's failure of an external inspection and now works part-time in an office doing clerical work. At the time she left her school:

Everyone said, 'Oh don't go – what a loss to the profession'. So I got given a nice plant at Christmas and that was it, I left – end of career as far as everyone was concerned.

She was really worried about getting another job doing anything because of the stigma. She said, 'I didn't want people to think I was a lousy teacher. I wondered if people would employ me if they knew I hadn't coped with teaching and was working in a school that had failed.'

She finds her new work frustrating but no longer has the stresses and strains of teaching:

I am a bit frustrated now because the job is the other end of the scale. I have gone from an alarming amount of responsibility to virtually none at all. I just do what I'm told and I'm doing a job you just leave behind at five o'clock.

Although engaging in very different work, Julie initially retained aspects of her teacher identity. She gave advice to workmates and friends about the education of their children and regarding some tasks in the office colleagues said, 'Oh, Julie's a teacher, she'll do that'.

Mary (fifty-two years) had returned to school after a two-term absence that she considered had been caused by the simultaneous intensification of her work and the violent and acrimonious breakdown of her relationship with her partner. In the first week of her return, the headteacher placed her on competency procedures because of complaints from parents concerning her lengthy absence and her alleged ineffectiveness as a class teacher. After a term in which she had to conform to the competency procedures but was frequently absent, she again left for extended sick leave. She now feels that it will be impossible for her to satisfy the school of her competence and has decided to leave teaching rather than go back to face further humiliation and stress. Having left under these circumstances, she feels that she will have to leave teaching altogether since transfer to another school would be difficult or impossible to achieve owing to her having to tell a potential employer about the competency procedures and receiving a negative reference from her current headteacher. Consequently, Mary felt 'forced out' of teaching.

For these teachers, their teaching careers are clearly at an end. Two of them, Marion and Ben, are suffering from a depressive illness and felt they could not return. Ben has become disillusioned with the concept and experience of 'career' no matter what the occupation. Return for Mary and Julie would involve overcoming major stigmas surrounding 'incompetency' and school 'failure' respectively, something they seemed unlikely to do.

Downshifting

Downshifting involved reducing workload, responsibilities and status. Some felt able to return to teaching after a break. Others departed radically from notions of 'objective' or 'normal' traditional career. Several teachers adjusted their 'working conditions and their degree of personal investment' to the job (Huberman, 1993: 153). All effectively were curtailing their careers. The ways they sought to modify their work took the form of *planned demotion, role-reduction, or role-redefinition*.

Planned demotion

This form involves the teacher voluntarily occupying a role that is lower in status than the one they are seeking to leave. This kind of adaptation involving, for instance, a headteacher moving vertically downwards in their career, to become a deputy headteacher, used to be an extremely rare phenomenon prior to the recent reforms (Woods, 1983).

Merryl (thirty-five years) had been a headteacher in a small school. She felt she was over-promoted and realised she could not fulfil the requirements of the role. She took a job as a deputy headteacher in a larger school following her illness and found this work less stressful and that it also comprised improved staff relationships:

> There are lots more people to share things with. I think one of my big things is that I'm not the final buffer. There's somebody else there as

well. The actual curriculum responsibilities are shared out because we've got fourteen staff. So instead of three of you doing nine subjects, there are fourteen of you doing nine subjects; and just generally the inter-action that you get as well.

However, there was stigma (Goffman, 1963) attached to her career change which threatened her identity:

> In the interview I was asked why I was going from a headship to a deputy headship. I just said honestly – well, of course I couldn't say I couldn't cope with headship. I said, 'I'd done my stint at my last school but I wasn't sure whether I was ready for another headship. So I wanted to step back a little bit and experience life in a larger school.' And it was truthful. I did want to move into a different situation just to try and analyse whether it was me or the job.
>
> I felt a bit of an anomaly when I met heads and deputies in part-nership schools at the beginning of term. They would say, 'Oh, you were a head weren't you? Oh, why did you become a deputy?' They kept asking *why*. I felt a bit like a talking point really.

The stigma, the previous experience of stress and lack of self-confidence in the headteacher role made it unlikely that Merryl would seek to (re)develop her career by seeking headteacher posts.

Role-reduction

Teachers adapting through role-reduction relinquished posts of responsi-bility and the payments that went with them. Unlike planned demotion, this form of adaptation was smaller in scale (i.e. a smaller step down) and was sometimes suggested or imposed by management as a condition of return to work. This mode of adaptation resulted in the teachers having to do less administrative work, like paperwork and attending meetings. The resulting reduction in role pressures while making life 'more bearable' in and out of school signalled a dilution in the role occupant's career. Role-reduction involves progressive 'disengagement' (Huberman, 1993).

William (forty-five years) returned to school after a depressive illness and reduced his several co-ordination roles and, while not experienc-ing stigma from the other teachers in the school (all female), found diffi-culties with relationships with some colleagues after relinquishing status and responsibilities (in charge of Science, Design and Technology, which carried a responsibility allowance; also doing Games and Audio-Visual Aids):

> A few weeks ago the person who'd taken my Science post was talking about reorganising the Science resources and in fact it was how it used

to be, how I used to have it, and I was told it had to change because we had this new room in school. And she said, 'I think we ought to do this, that and the other', and I just said something about, 'Well, we used to do that and I was told at the time that it had to change because that wasn't meeting the National Curriculum blah, blah, blah'. And somebody else said, 'But you must, William, let other people do their own, or make their own mistakes or have a go themselves'. And I was saying, 'Well I wasn't meaning it in an unpleasant way. I was just trying to save you time by doing something that perhaps wouldn't work'. But, as I say, basically I haven't volunteered for anything this term. I've just really kept my head down most of the time. I've just gone into school a bit later than I used to. I just do my job and mark the books more or less quite a lot of breaks and lunchtimes. I don't go in the staff room quite as much. I try to keep out of the way I suppose. I have to keep on top of all the marking. And then I don't run any clubs at all after school, which is the first time ever.

Feeling 'trapped' with many years to go until retirement, William's commitment is now one of 'career continuance' (Nias, 1980). He considers he is too old to retrain in an alternative occupation and too young to leave with a reasonable pension (he does not qualify for early retirement). William is attempting to 'sit it out' until retirement, but is finding that this strategy will probably be unsuccessful in the long term owing to the demands being made on all the teachers at his school for constant improvement.

Role-redefinition

Some of the teachers left full-time employment for part-time contracts or to work as supply teachers. While this was seemingly done voluntarily the teachers actually felt they had little choice. They could not continue in the role that had made them ill. By re-defining the role and reducing commitment these teachers no longer had the responsibility for: displays; being a subject co-ordinator; writing reports; writing curriculum programmes for the year; attending parents' evenings; attending curriculum meetings; and many of the other tasks they found stressful.

Olivia (fifty-eight years) left the school where she had felt 'bullied' by management and was appointed in another small school but this was a part-time fixed-term job rather than her previous full-time permanent contract.

Rita (forty-five years) left her school where she was undergoing competency procedures in order to do supply teaching:

I agonised because being the only breadwinner I have to earn enough money to pay the mortgage. But the job was making me ill. I thought I should work to live not the other way round. So I have a lot of friends who've gone into supply. I thought I would give up full-time teaching and go into supply.

Lorraine (thirty years) had been pressured to be a Music co-ordinator. Initially she refused the role though the school insisted. She said, 'They were so pleased to get me because I could play the piano, and Music co-ordinators are as rare as rocking horse droppings.' After a year in this post she found the work too demanding and had an extended sickness absence. She returned to her school and took a post as a 'floating' teacher. In this role, she covered for the other teachers to give them non-contact time or substituted when a member of staff was absent thus relinquishing the many duties of a class teacher.

As noted earlier, career breaks and returning to teaching as supply or temporary teachers have been part of the female teacher employment pattern for many years (Evetts, 1987; Acker, 1992). However, now, for some teachers, the reason for the break is illness rather than child rearing and the choice of supply or temporary work is not as a stepping stone to restart a career but an end in itself. Teaching may be becoming (re)feminised not only in being an occupation with a large female majority workforce, but in the sense that men are being offered or obliged to accept types of work and work conditions which women have always experienced in state schooling. This study supports Acker's finding that women teachers' careers are influenced by 'unexpected life events' and stressful work is a major factor in this respect. Additionally, it is not only women who are living through a crisis in careers. Men, too, are experiencing forced career breaks (and all that this entails in terms of getting back into teaching) or early termination of career. In the current climate of intensification and accountability (Jeffrey and Woods, 1998), changing schools, or making a 'gentle' return to teaching after a prolonged period of stress-related illness, is unlikely to be facilitated by the kinds of supportive informal networks of colleagues, headteachers and LEA described by Evetts (1987).

Self-actualising

A number of teachers laid emphasis on making the most of change by looking for opportunities for development or realisation of the self, and seeking new identities. The main means were through re-routeing or re-locating.

Re-routeing

Whereas retreatism involves 'little choice in the face of superior hostile forces', re-routeing is a 'positive act of removal or redirection' (Woods, 1995b: 9). Re-routeing involves 'finding new opportunities for lifelong ambitions'. It is a 'strategy to save and promote the self'. Even though transferring to new careers from teaching is difficult and some suffer occupational 'locking in' (Travers and Cooper, 1996) some of the teachers felt that they could no longer remain in teaching and, therefore, must re-route. This allowed them to preserve the values that they had previously invested in teaching.

Thomas (forty-six years), who had been prominent in creative and artistic education and at the forefront of progressive primary education throughout his career, was taking early retirement. After spending the past two years successfully getting his school off special measures (instituted by Ofsted inspectors because they had judged the school to be 'failing'), he resigned as headteacher after:

> giving considerable thought as to whether I wanted to be part of this any more. The experiences I have gone through in the past years have been so negative and have cost me so much personally that the answer is 'no'. I could no longer stomach the climate of blame that the harsh and unyielding system of school inspections had created. Not only is it stifling individuality and destroying teachers' self-confidence, it is driving many headteachers out and making headships increasingly difficult to fill.

With, potentially, a further twenty years to go in headship, his pupils' parents and his friends find it difficult to understand his decision:

> It was partly professional pride and also knowing the picture given by the inspection report was flawed. I was also determined not to be a victim. I look at parents and see the process that is going on. They're thinking, 'Is he cracking up? Is he just not up to it? Is it a mid-life crisis?' Friends cannot understand why I would want to leave a relatively well-paid job.

He refused to continue in headship and is beginning a new career as a writer of children's books and plays about schoolteachers. In this activity he can express his strong commitment to education in a wider sense, but faces the uncertainty involved in adopting the new role with poor financial prospects.

Barbara (forty-eight years), who was strongly committed to early years teaching in an inner city school, lost her father and her job (redundancy forced by school closure) in the same week. She explained that she had 'lost the two things she loved most', and her period of grieving for her father and her lost identity as a teacher (Nias, 1991) is currently continuing. She had experienced a breaking of the 'essential link' between a person's sense of identity and the work she performed (Berger, 1964). Recently she has been appointed as an educational liaison worker to work with mothers on an inner city housing estate to develop stronger relationships between school and home. In this way she can begin to redevelop the human relationships she found so important in her work as an infant teacher. However, the work is part-time and on a one-year contract basis. Consequently she is suffering insecurity as well as a major reduction in salary.

These teachers, although finding the curtailment of the teaching career painful, did have the 'luxury' of some measure of financial security (small pension – redundancy payment) to cushion their entry into and development of an alternative career which would allow reinvestment of their values.

Re-locating

Some of the teachers found self-fulfilment by re-locating to a different school and doing work more in line with their values (see Nias, 1989). Anna (twenty-five years) had difficulties in her previous school teaching KS 2 children and trying to fit into a hostile teacher culture. She found it easy to change schools (she had taught at three in her short career) because as a young teacher she was relatively inexpensive to employ. Her move enabled her to join a school staff to whom she thought she could relate more easily and teach nursery children with whom she felt more comfortable.

Vanessa (forty-five years) experienced stress in her work in a 'failing school' but did not have extended sick leave. She perceived the sources of her stress to be the intensification of her work and not being recognised as a good teacher by the management in the school. Despite the stigma of the 'failing' school label she was appointed as Humanities co-ordinator, which was a promotion, at another school. She described her new school and job as follows:

> I think the catchment area is a lot tougher and I am stressed, but now I can tell the difference between unhealthy stress and healthy stress. What I was suffering from was not a healthy form of stress. I think stress is part of life, it is definitely part of a teacher's life. In my present job I have bad times when I get in a panic and everything goes to hell in a basket but I'm doing fine. I'm really enjoying it.

Susan (thirty-three years) had not taken time off work even though she was stressed. This was because she did not want a 'stain' to be on her record and affect future appointments and planned on 'leaving in a dignified fashion'. She felt capable of continuing full-time by re-locating, an option not open to retreating and downshifting teachers. She found self-fulfilment by leaving a school with a culture of 'bureaucracy' and 'overwork' for more human relationships and part-time work which enabled her to spend more time with her daughter at home. Her commitment was now more towards herself and family than to school (Healy, 1999):

I think I said it in my letter of application. I was regrettably having to leave my job because I needed to spend time with my young daughter, which was perfectly true. And it's never ever been questioned. And in fact I had a conversation with him (headteacher) along those lines the other night. Not specifically talking about me. But how teaching doesn't tend to allow you to spend much time with your family. And I was saying that's exactly why I had to make this kind of decision. Because it was either be a teacher or be a parent. There didn't seem to be much in between. But fortunately I found this part-time job which is working out well. The financial side is dreadful, because you're working a small proportion of what you were, but it's a long way away and you're only doing two hours a day. . . . But it's done me the world of good in getting back to somewhere where they actually seem to be quite human . . . (for example) . . . in the way that they talk and they laugh. They seem to enjoy themselves.

She anticipated gradually building up to full-time work again as her daughter became older. In this way she could continue developing her career.

While it was the women who sought self-fulfilment in children and the family and reduced their commitment to work by changing it in the way Susan describes, some of the men coped with stressful work and gained self-fulfilment by increasing their commitment to activities outside school or home. Examples of this included voluntary youth work, voluntary administrative work in county cricket, playing tennis and frequent involvement at a religious social club.

George (forty-five years) found self-fulfilment by leaving his full-time job in teaching, which he had found stressful, in order to raise his children, while his wife who was employed on a series of short-term contracts as a lecturer became the principal breadwinner. Once the children reached school age he returned to teaching on supply in order to, 'use my capacity to earn as a supply teacher; that's the bits that make up the gaps. But I wouldn't take even a temporary full-time job. It's too much.' This lifestyle allows him to develop his interest in renovating vintage cars and attending car rallies. Although he 'takes work as it comes', he is prepared to return to teaching full-time if his wife's career falters.

This does not mean that we are witnessing the rise of a self-actualising generation of teachers that has been described by some writers (Hargreaves, 1994; Cherniss, 1995; Bartlett, 1998). Teachers faced with reinventing themselves and their careers are limited by more than just their aspirations. As Cherniss (1995: 166) explains:

People can make their lives better or worse, but what they think, how they feel and what they do are strongly shaped by the social contexts in which they live.

Conclusion

In the light of the evidence presented in this chapter, the notion of 'career' needs reconceptualising. Certainly 'objective career' theory and research, even though it briefly touches on early leavers and 'wastage' to the profession, does not engage with the types of adaptations and their consequences described in this study. Many of the teachers in the sample also appeared to lack the degree of agency and control which is emphasised in theories on 'subjective careers', suggesting that these theories may also be in need of development.

Teaching, for many, is no longer a job for life. The notion of a career being hierarchical (in terms of moving vertically upwards) and continuous to the age of sixty or sixty-five years of age is breaking down. Many careers are now fragmented by the forced interruptions of redundancy, early retirement or breakdown retirement. Increasingly careers are becoming discontinuous or experienced on a plateau or involving vertical movement downwards through strategies of downshifting (Sennett, 1998). In conditions of turbulence and anxiety teachers face these insecurities largely unprepared and alone. Macnicol (1999: 30) argues that 'being continually exposed to such risks eats away at one's sense of character; the destruction of personal narratives by which people make sense of their past engenders confusion and alienation'.

Perhaps change is necessary to remove some of the ineffective and inefficient teachers from the system in order to accelerate improvement in educational provision? The replacement of older teachers with younger, cheaper, more instrumentally committed, compliant and malleable ones well versed in the National Curriculum may be the answer. Indeed, Her Majesty's Chief Inspector of Schools with his idea of dismissing fifteen thousand incompetent teachers (Woodhead, 1995: 15) may be seeking not only to remove the type of teachers he considers a hindrance to educational progress, but also to use the threat of sacking in order to gain greater control of those teachers who remain in the system. It may be, of course, that it is this public 'discourse of derision' (Ball, 1994), and images of the stressful and discontinuous career that make teaching an increasingly unattractive proposition to potential recruits.

Whatever the intention, the result is a huge personal cost to some teachers and to the education system in general. The system suffers in terms of the loss of experienced teachers and the money that was invested in their skills and knowledge in terms of training and staff development. This cultural and economic loss is increased considerably if sick pay, redundancy payments, pensions and in some cases compensation payments are added. Further, there is evidence that the profession may be losing some of its best teachers. Woods (1990: 185), for instance, argues that for some teachers:

redefinition or adaptation, for some reason or another, is difficult, painful, or impossible. Among these are those teachers who are highly committed, vocationally oriented and 'caring', for there is no escape route open to them. They will not weaken their commitment. There is nothing left to give way but themselves. The best teachers, arguably, are the most vulnerable.

The data on which this chapter is based gives insights into the personal and social consequences of change. Rapid and wide-ranging changes in the nature of teachers' work are producing conditions of uncertainty in which traditions and social structures are crumbling (Giddens, 1991; Jeffrey, 1998), and the tension and interplay between the global and local are experienced. Giddens (1991: 5) argues that:

> One of the distinctive features of (high) modernity is an increasing interconnection between the two extremes of extensionality and intentionality. Globalising influences on the one hand and personal dispositions on the other. . . . The more tradition loses its hold, and the more daily life is reconstituted in terms of the dialectical interplay of the local and the global, the more individuals are forced to negotiate lifestyle choices among a diversity of options. . . . Reflexively organized life-planning . . . becomes a central feature of the structuring of self-identity.

In the conditions of late modernity planning becomes more difficult as traditional social and cultural landmarks disappear and nothing stands still. However, individuals in these circumstances cannot choose not to choose, for in the absence of traditional status passages and attendant rites of passage they have to continually re-invent themselves (Woods, 1999a). For many of the phases in the unpredictable new career there are no scripts which people can follow (Ford, 1992). Careers must be negotiated and re-negotiated repeatedly. Lifestyle choices involving the re-invention of identity are recurring aspects of late modernity and the demise of the regularised society. Making these choices in the circumstances described in this chapter is, of course, a highly constrained, convoluted and stressful process in itself. As Woods (1983: 160) points out, 'career structures cannot be re-formulated in one's head over-night'.

The head of the governmental organisation responsible for teacher supply has recently announced that 'people should be encouraged to spend just a few years teaching during more flexible and varied careers' (Barnard, 1999: 1). He clearly recognises the physically, psychologically and emotionally demanding nature of teaching in contemporary schooling and seems to have in mind co-opting teaching personnel, on a temporary basis, from other occupations, when he says that:

We have to make it possible for people to come in and give some very enthusiastic, energetic years. There's a bit of teacher in all of us ... we can do quite well to get people fired up to teach for ten years of their career rather than the whole thing.

One wonders what kind of teacher will be recruited to the 'officially' discontinuous career. Will they be the kind of stress-proofed technicians that Jeffrey and Woods (1996) describe driven by instrumental commitment at the outset? And what will happen to those vocationally oriented teachers who thought they had chosen a career for life once they are burned out after a decade? Currently there is no provision for teachers to change career 'escalators' (Strauss, 1971), either by re-training for work in a different phase of education (this is possible in Scotland) or in a new occupation. Further, the measures the policy makers have devised so far do little to change the conditions of teachers' work to make them less stressful and supportive of career development and workplace commitment (Rosenholtz, 1989) – rather the reverse. For example, the zero-tolerance policy of school 'improvement' by 'naming, blaming and shaming' schools that are judged to be 'failing', has been a major source of teacher stress and impetus for early exit for all kinds of teachers, 'failing' or not (see Chapter 2). The break-up of the teacher career as it has been known seems set to continue.

5 Coping with stress

Introduction

Most of our sample were older teachers who had, throughout their careers, developed successful coping strategies to deal with everyday constraints which had become part of their jobs, such as the state of school buildings, class size, salary levels or recalcitrant pupils. However, they had had to confront a number of new constraints inherent in intensification, managerialism and the new accountability systems, and these demanded new coping strategies (Giddens, 1991). For some of our sample these strategies were successful and enabled them to continue in teaching, to enjoy and benefit from their professional lives, their selves intact. For the majority, however, they were unsuccessful, and these teachers left their jobs with damaged selves and 'spoiled careers' (Goffman, 1968).

The concept of 'coping strategy' in relation to teaching was developed in the 1970s. Hargreaves (1978) argued that what had to be coped with had macro-structural origins – as in this case with the restructuring of the educational system. However, these 'societal demands' are then mediated through institutional goals and constraints (Hargreaves, 1978). Woods (1979) focused on those aspects of the self that interacted with practical difficulties of the job, setting up a process of 'accommodation'. In extreme circumstances, these produced a range of 'survival strategies', where the aim was survival – continuance in post, getting through the day, week, year without giving way to stress or illness – rather than teaching as such. Some survival strategies, in fact, run counter to teaching. Pollard (1982) codified and developed this work. Acknowledging the structural factors, he drew attention, firstly, to the importance in coping stategies of the negotiated classroom micro-structure between teachers and pupils, teacher culture, and the 'institutional bias'. Secondly, Pollard laid emphasis on the importance of the 'self' in coping. After all, not all teachers in the same situation react in the same way. Some might feel enhanced in fact, while others feel pressurised; and of the latter, some might cope, others suffer burnout. Thus we need to know 'what particular conception of 'self' teachers hold so that we can document the purposes or goals of their adaptation' (ibid.: 28). This takes us into teacher biography, their perception of their role, and a consideration of their 'interests-at-hand', such as 'issues of self-image, work-load, health and stress, enjoyment, autonomy, order and instruction' (ibid.: 32). Pollard argues that teachers typically 'juggle' these interests 'to achieve a satisfactory balance for self-interests overall' (ibid.). The value of Pollard's model lies in its development of the significance of 'self' within an integrated view of the influence of structural, institutional and personal factors on the origins and development of coping strategies.

We have seen the importance of many of these in previous chapters. For instance, the strategies used by the teachers in the failing school case study in Chapter 2 to maintain their selves, and the career adjustments made by the teachers in Chapter 4. In this chapter, using examples of the coping strategies commonly used by the members of our sample of teachers, we illustrate another general feature of coping strategies – the matter of countervailing power and the generation of resources to support it. Coping is a matter of retaining or regaining a measure of personal control of one's actions in the face of threats of destabilisation. It is a case of gathering strength. But whence does this derive? The individual seems almost powerless in the face of government and institutional pressure, particularly in these prescriptive times. Our material suggests at least three sources at three different levels – the self, others, and the group. There is a kind of symmetry here in reflecting the constraints. If the constraints derive in large measure from macro-structure, are mediated by the institution and negotiated by the self, then with respect to our data at least coping takes place, in the first instance, at the level of the self, calling on one's own personal resources; then more generally at institutional level through alliances with others; and finally through the group rather than the self. The latter has referents at the structural, societal level, being associated, in our analysis, with the rise of new social movements replacing the trade unions of old. In these ways a form of power is generated from below, as it were (Kreisberg, 1992), to counteract the exertion of power from above that has served to destabilise the situation for particular teachers.

We consider examples from the three main areas of generating and using personal resources, seeking alliances, and group formation. These are not entirely discrete categories, nor, of course, do they take place neatly in sequence. Stress results from an aberration in life. There are no programmes to handle it as in structured status passages (Ford, 1992), and coping with it can be a difficult, messy affair. Categorising gives us some purchase on the major elements, if not the total process, of the experience.

Generating and using personal resources

Strategies used here included *distancing, self-determining, regaining perspective and balance,* and *reading and writing.*

Distancing

An early task is to neutralise the assaults on self, recharge the self, and rediscover one's identity as a person that one recognises and esteems. A common method of doing this for our teachers was to remove themselves from and to avoid the social situations which they perceived to have caused their illness, and to seek situations which promised a more positive self-image. This involved distancing by withdrawing from the school during long periods of illness. The women in our sample expressed fear on approaching the school during the onset of their illness. Lorraine recalls the emotions of this period:

> I remember driving to school in the mornings even if it wasn't sunny, with my sunglasses on, with tears streaming down my face, thinking if I didn't have Rosie (daughter) in this car because she goes to the same school as I teach at, I'd just drive straight past. And it was a physical feeling of just not wanting to be there. And these kids because they were just starting school, were crying and clinging to their mums and dads and screaming and I was thinking, 'I want to do that'. This is what I want to do. I want to be cuddled and just taken away from this place.

Mary felt like a 'school phobic and I now know how those kids feel' but 'you shouldn't be feeling like that as an adult'. Jackie experienced 'panic attacks' prior to her illness and withrew from school during it:

> I used to drive into work and my stomach would be churning. I'd feel nauseous. You'd feel as though you were ready to throw up – a dry mouth, a panic attack. When I was away from work I couldn't go anywhere near the school. I couldn't go anywhere near the roads that led into the school. I would take a detour rather than go near it.

During illness some of the teachers left the areas of their homes to be alone or with members of their family. Tony visited his parents in Northumberland. William borrowed a friend's flat in Chester. Jackie accompanied her sister-in-law: 'I went down to Sussex to visit my other brother who is a teacher – just to get away from the area and clear my head.'

Withdrawing from the workplace, and being freed of its pressures, enabled Jackie to focus on herself and her predicament:

> I used to go for really long walks in the park with another teacher who was ill and talk about things. It was just being able to talk to somebody, I think. It helps you to rationalise what's going on in your head. Because when I was at work I was so busy working and rushing around I was going in ever decreasing circles and not really thinking about

anything. I wasn't able to really concentrate on what was happening to me. It was like an *Alice in Wonderland* life. Being off I was actually able to sort out what was important and what wasn't important. And just getting time, I think, to straighten myself out helped.

Withdrawing from the workplace allowed some of the teachers to have some freedom and rediscover themselves by taking up new activities which were important for positive self-image, relaxation and renewal (cf. Marion's 'normal' and 'abnormal' life in Chapter 4). Mary explains that, while absent from work,

> I had a really wonderful time being a person. In the September term I went to some Workers' Education Authority history classes, I went to the Women's Institute and I was going out and doing all sorts of things. And I've learnt what life could be like if you're not teaching and if all you're doing is getting up, getting to school by half past eight, doing a day's work at school, coming home, making yourself a meal or doing another evening's school work then. I found out what life was about. And I didn't want to go back to the stresses of teaching. You just feel so fraught all the time. You've got so many pressures on you and trying to do this, trying to do that, being told, 'Oh you mustn't do group work', or 'You must do whole class teaching', and 'This is wrong', and 'That's wrong'. We're in a no win situation. Whatever we do is wrong.

Not being at school, apart from providing time for reflection, also enabled the teachers to engage in tasks that improved their self-image and confidence. For instance, Jackie used her English teaching skills and knowledge to help a neighbour's son:

> I took on a little lad who was dyslexic, whose mother wanted me to help him. And I started tutoring him. And I got such a good response I felt I can't be that bad.

This experience, together with helping out at her daughter's drama group with rehearsals, was instrumental in raising her self-esteem, thus allowing her to return to work.

William withdrew from school during long-term illness. On his return he distanced himself physically from potentially stressful situations in the school by avoiding the staffroom and main school areas during breaks. He referred to this as 'keeping a low profile' and 'keeping his head down'.

Self-determining

If one is to succeed in coping, the desire has to be there. The large majority of our sample were resolute about overcoming their illness and returning to work. Many felt a strong sense of injustice at what had happened to them and were determined not only to 'get mad' but also to 'get even'. Olivia asked, 'How dare they make me ill'. At fifty-nine years old she was offered early retirement but refused it arguing that she loved the job and also 'wanted to see justice'. Mary was 'determined to make an effort' because she felt she was not an 'old stick-in-the-mud', and was:

> prepared to go in to school and tough it out with her (headteacher) the next term. I went in fighting fit to do that and a couple of the staff to whom I've spoken have said, 'We can't understand why you are now ill because you went in and you were so positive at the beginning of term'. And I was. I thought, 'They're not going to get the better of me'. I'd gone back so positive thinking: 'I'm going to beat them, they're not going to get me on this competency procedure'.

William saw himself as a 'victim' of bullying but had a 'fighter's instinct' and was sure that he 'was not going to let her (i.e. his headteacher) win' and was intending to ride the storm. Jeremy 'drew on the strengths of his reserves' in order to return to work. He felt he was 'not the sort to just walk away from something' because he would feel that he 'had left things unfinished'. Jackie saw returning to school as a way of 'getting back' at the headteacher who had been bullying her:

> I just got the idea that I wasn't going to let them put me down. I think I must have just been coming out of my depression. I thought, 'Well, it's very easy to give up', and say, 'No, I can't do it'. But I got into an angry mood and I thought the last thing they want is for me to go back. It would be just what he wants, for me not to go back. So I thought, 'Well, I'll go back'.

Jackie, upon returning to work after illness, was determined to combat the bullying techniques of her headteacher:

> I asked to have an interview with him and be accompanied by the occupational health manager. And we sort of set up a little agreement, of things that we thought would be fair. And one of the things that I asked was that I could have a meeting for five or ten minutes every week just to check how things were going. And if he had any complaints he could make them then. He said, 'Yes, that would be fine'. And then he invited this other woman, that had taken my job as year co-ordinator, to one of the meetings – talk about rubbing my nose in it! And I thought, 'Right, two can play at that game'. So I said, 'Well I'll take my union representative' because the head had actually misquoted something I'd said at a previous meeting when I hadn't had represen-tation. And he wrote down some minutes saying things that hadn't

been said. So I thought, 'Right, from now on I'm not going to have a meeting with you on my own again'. And that really put him on the spot. Because I wouldn't ever have a conversation with him without somebody else there. I did take advice on a lot of things. And I read and I read and I read. Everything there was to read about stress and everything there was to read about being assertive, being positive and pulling yourself out of it.

Regaining perspective and balance

The experience of illness threw life out of balance for the teachers. Part of the recovery process was to re-prioritise aspects of their lives. Jeremy concluded, as a result of his illness, that he had previously had an unbalanced view, in which work was the main priority. He now held the view that teaching was 'only a job – not a way of life'. Jackie also had been led to realise that other areas of her life demanded her attention:

> As a family we've had a very difficult time because my husband's first family had three children, and the older girl died of leukaemia just a week before Christmas. Completely out of the blue and knocked us all for six. Very, very difficult. But it tends to put everything in perspective a bit. When you've got a major stress like that you begin to think other things just don't hurt you so much. You toss them off and think, 'Well, we seem to be coming out of it quite well now'. I've been preparing for Ofsted, had the car stolen and all the hassle with the insurance company and my husband's daughter dying. As a family we were devastated with all these things. Work now has improved so much with the new regime that it is almost a stable in your life that you can turn to.

Judith's GP advised her to restore her balance in life:

> She gave me things to do, which I needed. Something that I could feel I was doing. Making lists of the things that I felt had contributed to the way I was feeling. And then making lists of all the things that I used to do before I felt I was working all the time, which was quite horrendous because I discovered that I wasn't doing any of them any more – sort of hobby things like painting, sewing, I would play the violin. I hadn't played the violin for ages. And so she made me pick one activity. In fact she more or less pointed me in the direction of one that was not too threatening to get back into. And said, 'Right, you're going to do that between now and when I see you. You're going to do it'. In fact it was making a skirt. But it was something concrete to actually do. And it was something that I'd always enjoyed because I did like doing creative things and I hadn't had the time, or I felt I

hadn't had the time. So I'd let all that go. So those were the sorts of things that she discussed with me – I suppose getting things into perspective, getting back in balance a bit.

Tony, a headteacher who had previously been bullied by the chair of governors, used time management and assertiveness in order to break down his intense focus on his work (at the expense of other areas of his life) and his obsessive perfectionism:

> I tend not to worry so much about being a perfectionist. I'm by nature a perfectionist. But now I think I'm prepared to let things slide a little bit more. Which could be the compromise with the policy documents. I'm not going for perfection in the policy documents but still trying to preserve the collegiality and ownership of something. But I'm not trying to have it perfect. And I think I've been able to shrug my shoulders and say, 'No. That's all the time I've got for it'. It's time management. I say to myself, 'You've given a lot of time to it and that's all you can do'. The occupational health manager told me about saying, 'No', to people and I've developed that strategy as well. There is one governor who asked me to do the health and safety policy, a carol service and the Christmas party all in the same week. So I told him where to go. And the daft thing was then he totally forgot about what he'd asked me after that – after the holidays. And we never got it all done. And I haven't worried about it.

Reading and writing

Many of the teachers read books and articles on stress and its management in magazines and professional journals. There are many forms of this type of publication available (see for example Cockburn (1996) *Teaching Under Pressure*). The bullied teachers benefited from reading *Bully in Sight* by Field (1996). Some teachers used the publication *Beating Stress at Work* (Woodham, 1995) which is produced by the Health Education Authority and on its cover invites the reader to:

*   examine your current lifestyle;
*   self-test your present level of psychological fitness;
*   improve your stress management.

In the early stages of illness, reading was difficult owing to poor concentration. However, once this period was over, most read voraciously. Reading, by providing a 'bigger picture', served the purpose of reassuring the individuals that they were not alone and also provided possible coping strategies. Jackie, who had been bullied by her headteacher, felt empowered by her reading and 'more in control'. The knowledge she acquired increased her self-confidence and security and she was able to construct a 'cocoon' (Giddens, 1991) to protect herself against further challenges to the self: 'I felt I had a shield round me really. He couldn't get to me. There was no way he could.'

Writing was equally, if not more, therapeutic. Some kept a diary, a model of which was provided in the stress management literature, enabling them to chart the trajectory of their illness and identify symptoms of stress as they arose. This facilitated the deployment of coping strategies at key times. William wrote poetry, something he did not normally do. These were explorations of fantasies of loss in love, providing an allegory for his loss of identity, status and skills as a teacher. Thomas wrote a play about the negative encroachment of managerialism in a primary school and the stressful impact this was having on the leading character, a progressive female teacher. Those teachers who were being bullied kept voluminous files of records of bullying incidents and notes and memos of what 'changeling' headteachers had said and done in meetings with them. Some took a professional 'friend' to these meetings to take minutes and offer emotional support. This documentation was, in some cases, to serve as evidence in an industrial tribunal or disciplinary hearing. Jackie explained that during her bullying:

> I put everything down, I just logged everything. I was logging everything that happened. And everything I felt was significant there's a memo for. I was using a photocopier. And I kept minutes and logs and records of everything that happened. And I did absolutely everything by the book. There was absolutely nothing that he could get me on. I went through all the channels, made sure I'd covered myself every way.

Seeking alliances

A range of 'social' coping strategies were used by the teachers. Jackie, when asked to explain one of the main ways she coped, said: 'I think it's other people. If I'd been on my own, totally on my own, I don't think I could have hacked it.'

Support was enlisted from medical professionals, colleagues, family and trade union officials.

Medical professionals

The entire core sample sought support from their GPs. The extent to which this enabled them to cope was valuable. Some of the doctors were reported as being excellent in the areas of diagnosis, advice and treatment. Jeremy said, 'My doctor was brilliant because he said he'd seen too much of this coming in from teaching, far too much of it.' Judith's GP, in addition to prescribing drugs and arranging counselling with a counsellor employed by the practice, also offered a lot of practical advice and sympathy which Judith judged to be of the right sort:

> She was really very, very good. Or at least I felt she was at the time because she wasn't over sympathetic which I was finding I couldn't handle.

It was her GP who suggested the coping strategies listed above (see Regaining perspective and balance, p. 99). The GP, at Judith's initial consultation, refused to let her leave the surgery until she had telephoned a union official to discuss the professional problems the GP said were making her ill. This GP referred to her school as a 'toxic workplace'.

By way of contrast, some GPs seemed unaware of the serious impact stress was having on their patients. One GP of the 'socks up school' (Wolpert, 1999) recommended Marion to 'pull her socks up' and advised her to cure sleeplessness problems and chronic headaches by taking a brisk walk round the block before retiring for the night! Marion was later diagnosed at a psychiatric hospital for clinical depression. General practitioners, such as Marion's, reluctant to support sick leave, tended to recommend an early return to work, arguing that being back at work would take the patient's mind off things, not acknowledging work as the source of the problem.

The entire core sample had visited the occupational health manager (a nurse trained in occupational health). Most found this beneficial because she was able to provide counselling support from a team of counsellors deployed throughout the authority (the local authority provided six one-hour sessions free), offer a wider perspective and do some confidence building. Merryl explained that:

> The occupational health manager was very good because she listened and she made me feel as though there was something wrong that wasn't my fault. That she'd seen the situation before.

The occupational health manager could suggest coping strategies and, since she knew employment law, was able to offer advice on, for instance, early retirement. She was also aware of micro-political situations in schools within the LEA and intervened (often by enlisting the support of LEA advisers) on behalf of individuals or groups of teachers on such matters as organisational sources of stress. She negotiated with headteachers about organisational, task and workload changes that would need to be made to enable a return to work (for example, staged returns).

Only one teacher raised doubts about the efficacy of the occupational health manager. He felt that she had divided loyalties and too often seemed to be taking the side of the local authority (particularly the personnel department). Indeed, the occupational health manager acknowledged that this role conflict was a source of stress in her own work. However, she did argue that her prime responsibility was with the teachers. The majority of teachers in our sample felt they had received unequivocal support from occupational health managers.

Although cognitive therapy is commonly used in the treatment of depression, of all the teachers diagnosed as having it, only two received this form of therapy. Both reported that they had benefited from the technique, enabling them to achieve some control in social situations in which they had previously felt powerless and anxious. The majority said they had benefited from counselling. Ben, however, said it had 'been a waste of time' and stopped attending after the second session. He found it difficult to relate to the 'personality' of the male counsellor who he also felt, as a non-teacher, could not understand the issues involved. Susan didn't take it up because

> I knew exactly what was happening and I didn't need help to see what my problem was. The occupational health manager said, 'Counselling is designed to help you see what the problem is and what you can do about it'. And I knew that. I'd worked that one out for myself. I didn't need somebody to sit there and say, 'Well what do you think the problem is?' I wanted to find out what I could do about it. The unfortunate thing is not a lot.

William had been admitted to a psychiatric hospital the day of his 'breakdown'. He returned as an out-patient and undertook a course of group therapy sessions which he found useful.

The entire core sample had been prescribed anti-depressants by their GPs. This was most often *Prozac*, a new generation drug of wide popularity (Stone, 1997). For some this was inappropriate and they were moved on to other types of anti-depressant. Some spent months having their dosage regulated which added to the stress they were experiencing (Wolpert, 1999). Of the core sample, most were prescribed drugs as a strategy to cope with depression while absent from school. The remainder were prescribed drugs to help them continue in teaching. The majority of the teachers relied upon the drugs in order to cope both in their professional and private lives. A minority rejected them because they saw the problem as being external to themselves. Dosages were reduced gradually as teachers returned to work, as they were 'weaned off' the medication. However, some teachers remained dependent on the drugs.

Stress is often coped with by the use/abuse of other drugs such as tobacco and alcohol, or by 'comfort eating' (Travers and Cooper, 1996). However, to our knowledge, only one teacher (female) in our sample smoked and she did not report increased levels of smoking. One male's alcohol consumption had risen and was causing a problem since, as he acknowledged, this increased his already aggressive behaviour. Generally, as far as it was possible for us to judge, the use of drugs of this type did not seem to be part of the coping strategies of our respondents.

Colleagues

Ben received no support from his colleagues when absent and he subsequently did not return to teaching. He was particularly hurt that his headteacher did not phone or call round to see him to enquire about his health. She would merely phone to request that he submit sick notes at the right time. This headteacher also ignored Ben when, during his absence from school, he attended a school carol service in which his own children were taking part. In some schools where stress pervaded the whole staff, the teachers were in some cases too pressurised themselves to support their colleagues. On Jeremy's return to school he found that, 'Some people on the staff would just give me a guarded nod, some wondered why I'd come back'. Stress further eroded staff relationships:

> I didn't want to see the other staff. You couldn't go in there and simply do a teaching job. It became a nightmare. To see people coming into the staff area crying – a man crying and shaking – somebody else getting in a car and driving away and not coming back. It wasn't a job any more.

However, in other schools there was a form of 'solidarity' (Jeffrey and Woods, 1998) amongst the teachers. In Jackie's school, for instance, some of the staff coped by giving and receiving emotional support:

> There were two who were still at school, one who was also off on a long-term sickness at the same time as me. The two who were still at school kept in touch with me up to a point and talked to me as though I was going to be able to come back, but whenever I was ready. They made me feel as though it wasn't my fault, that things were still going on that were bad, even after I had gone, that the pattern was the same. And they were actually suffering as well. So sharing and empathising I would say was what the people at work did. And we used to meet for coffee and maybe have a drink on a fortnightly basis. Something like that just to sort of say everything will be all right.

Olivia enlisted the support of two LEA advisers who could vouch for her professional acumen when she appeared at a disciplinary hearing:

> The English Adviser and the Personal and Social Education (PSE) Adviser who I'd approached supported me in what I'd been doing with the kids. And I went to see them during the period that I was off sick. And the PSE Adviser said to me she would be prepared to put it in writing to support me, not just in words, but in writing.

Tony felt confident enough to ask for support from the Regional Education Officer responsible for his school. This official did not view Tony's admission of stress as an indication that he was incompetent and could not cope in the headteacher role. He gave practical support on time management techniques in order to support Tony on his return to school.

Some of the teachers were supported by ancillary staff rather than teaching colleagues. William, who had withdrawn from interaction with his teaching colleagues and headteacher in the staffroom, would spend breaks from teaching with the caretaker (the only other male in the school) and with the cook in the school kitchen. At Mary's stressed school her main source of support was an LSA:

> The teachers were stressed out themselves. I had a card and a bunch of flowers and the occasional phone call. But actually the person who kept in touch with me and relayed messages to and fro was my nursery nurse.

Tracey's LSAs had become close friends who knew her so well they could spot warning signs of stress when they arose:

> I've got two classroom assistants (LSAs) who work with me but they've actually ended up being my closest friends as well. So we've got a good team there. And they're the people that actually see me, and know when I've been overdoing things or when work is infringing on my social life.

Pupils and parents

Poor relationships with pupils' parents can often be a source of stress in teaching (Hargreaves, 1999a). Generally the teachers did not cope by enlisting the support of parents of children in their classes. While Mary had received help from two parents this did not compensate for the number who had complained about her for her long absence and subsequent performance. She explained that, 'the bad news is too much – two drops in an ocean doesn't make up for the crashing waves'.

However, a number of teachers were helped to cope by their pupils. Joyce, for example, found that:

> At the end of the day the children are the only thing that keep me going. I mean they're lovely. The first day I went back in to visit, the supply teacher with my class said, 'I've never known children keep on about their teacher as much'. And they all threw their arms round me and those that couldn't get to me were sort of cuddling each other. So I felt that the children are the only thing that keep me going through it.

Teachers rarely see the end product of their labours. This can be a source of stress in teaching (Hargreaves, 1994) when tasks are endless and without reward. Jackie found the emotional bond she had with a former pupil impacted positively on her self-esteem:

> I'd met a former pupil in the doctor's waiting room and he'd been so nice, so good to me, about his plans for the future and how well he was getting on, as though he expected me to really care about him and be very interested. And I thought somebody thinks something of me because at that time my image of myself was about six inches tall. I'd completely lost my confidence in myself. And it was purely coincidence that this lad came up and spoke to me. But it made me feel as though he thought I was quite an important person.

Family

Support from the family was central to coping for the teachers. They received both emotional and practical support from this source. It was generally the teachers' partners who persuaded them to seek medical and professional help with the onset of illness. Jackie would probably not have returned to teaching if it had not been for her mother who:

> . . . was really very annoyed. She said, 'I think that it's such a terrible waste. You've trained – you can't be a bad teacher because you've been managing to do really well up till recently.' So it's a case of, 'Don't blame yourself'. And it took a long time, but gradually with a lot of support and encouragement and help, I began to think maybe I could try to return.

Some male partners took responsibility for household tasks for which they had not been responsible before; for example, cooking, washing, cleaning, shopping and paying bills. In some cases children would assume practical and emotional responsibilities normally carried out by the stressed parent (Carlyle, 1998). Some of the male partners were proactive and would accompany their partners to school meetings with the headteacher to discuss workplace issues which were contributing to stress. One male partner became politicised and set up a national helpline to support and campaign for the partners of stressed teachers (Sears, 1998). Jackie's brother provided security and reassurance:

> My brother is an ex bank manager and he likes to get to the bottom of things. He invited me over and talked to me about it, asked me questions, tried to get it clear in his mind. He said, 'Well, from an employer's point of view you haven't done this and you haven't done that.' Just to make sure that everything was all right, and that I hadn't

really done anything to be blamed for. And then once he had established in his own mind that I hadn't really done anything untoward he was very, very supportive. Strangely enough he didn't talk to me about the problem very much but he just gave me somewhere to be where I could be at peace with no stresses. So I think everybody helped me in their own different way. Part of it was providing a secure place where I could be, where I was welcomed and respected and cared for. Part of it was being interested in me as a professional person. Taking me seriously.

One male teacher, however, found that his partner was unable to offer commitment and support throughout his illness and subsequent unemployment. In this case his wife felt very guilty at not being able to continue fulfilling a 'normal' caring role, and when she withdrew the little emotional and practical support she was offering, the marriage broke down.

Union officials

Jackie found her school trade union representative very supportive:

My school union rep was very good. He kept trying to find out what exactly the head and chair of governors were up to – why they were trying to continue with this disciplinary action – because it could have easily been resolved. He wasn't getting very far with it but just kept on the pressure.

And the full-time national official also gave good practical support:

The union official, especially in the early stages, was really very good because he virtually said, 'I'll deal with this paperwork', and 'I'll sort this out, and if anything can be done I'll make sure I'll do it'. He seemed to be there for me.

However, the majority of bullied teachers (including one facing competency proceedings) did not receive strong support from their trade union officials. Mary found that in a meeting with her headteacher where charges were made about her alleged incompetency the union official, who was present at the meeting, agreed with the headteacher that Mary was incompetent. However, Mary felt it was difficult to see how the union official could reach his decision as he had only been familiar with the school, and Mary's case, for half-an-hour.

It seemed usual in such cases for union officials to recommend early retirement on grounds of ill-health. There often seemed to be a division of loyalty here concerning the union official's line of responsibility – the LEA, the school or the union member (Wragg et al., 1998).

Collective action: re-establishing power and identity

The failure of the unions to provide meaningful assistance led to five of our respondents setting up a self-help group to support teachers who, like them, had been 'bullied' at work. These teachers felt they had been, or were being, forced out of teaching, were experiencing stress-related illness and felt marginalised, alienated and powerless. They had been ignored or felt inadequately supported by their trade unions when requesting professional help and support with workplace problems. Consequently they had a great deal of 'resentment against (their) unfair exclusion' (Castells, 1997: 9).

It will be seen that the 'coping' here has been taken to a new level – that of the group, one that can be equated with others in a trend among occupations in general. The emergence of such groups is interpreted by some (see for example Offe, 1990: 246–7) as a reaction to the 'poverty of public policy to solve some of society's most pressing problems'. While the growth of environmental, peace and women's movements is clear in British society, it is accompanied by a burgeoning of smaller single issue support groups. For example, a directory of national self-help groups available on the Internet (Garril, 1998) lists a total of 700 groups alphabetically from *Action on Elder Abuse* to *Worster-Drought Syndrome Contact Group.* Anti-bullying at work groups exist in the UK (*Suzy Lamplugh Trust, Andrea Adams Trust, Redress, Freedom to Care*), in Italy, France, Netherlands, Sweden and Germany. In Finland, *Kiusattujen Tukiry,* a national group, was created in 1983 for bullied schoolchildren, but now seeks to serve the needs of bullied teachers. There are at least two websites (see for example http://www.successunlimited.co.uk) devoted to combating bullying in the workplace, one of which has an international mailbase. In England and Wales the DfEE has recently set up a telephone helpline for stressed teachers. The Trades Union Congress in addition to its helpline has publicised the issue of workplace bullying through such campaigns as *Bad Boss Week.* While this is an issue of which trade unions are clearly aware, their powers to deal with it have been severely curtailed since the widespread industrial unrest and actions of the mid 1980s. Castells (1997: 354), for example, argues that given the decline in trade union powers it is left to margin-alised groups to reinvent collectivity and collective protest. He argues that:

> The privatisation of the public agencies and the demise of the welfare state, while alleviating societies from some bureaucratic burden, worsen living conditions for the majority of citizens, break the historic social contract between capital, labour, and the state, and remove much of the social safety net, the nuts and bolts of legitimate government for common people. Torn by internationalisation of finance and produc-tion, unable to adapt to networking of firms and individualisation of work, and challenged by the degendering of employment, the labour

movement fades away as a major source of social cohesion and workers' representation. It does not disappear, but it becomes primarily a political agent integrated into the realm of public institutions. . . . The institutions and organisations in civil society that were constructed around the democratic state, and around the social contract between capital and labour, have become, by and large, empty shells, decreasingly able to relate to people's lives and values in most societies.

Geoff was invited to join the group as someone who they knew had understanding of and sympathy for their position, and who could, potentially, publicise their plight and perhaps influence policy on bullying in the workplace. Geoff attended their monthly evening meetings over a period of a year, at first in a pub and later in a rented hall. The first meeting took place in a hall that had hosted both a major non-conformist religious group in the seventeenth century and also the inaugural meeting of a 1940s humanitarian charity group which subsequently developed into an eco-movement. This immediately alerted us to the possibility of the emergence of a new social movement. In what follows, we adopt the conventional conceptual areas of new social movements analysis by considering the ideology, participants, structure and strategies of the teacher self-help group.

Ideology

The source of the group's disaffection lay in breaches of trust and negative workplace relationships. Here was the classic schism between 'us' and 'them' characteristic of conflicts between capital and labour manifest in negative industrial relations. The twin aims of the teachers' self-help group had a political and personal orientation which fused into one: they were to engage in the political process of confronting employers and unions about their plight and seek some form of redress while also offering emotional and practical support to members. Many members who had experienced prolonged 'bullying' had sustained physical, psychological and emotional damage. Thus, the group had the differing goals attending a 'power' orientation on the one hand, and an 'identity' orientation on the other (Rucht, 1990). The former orientation, however, was largely concerned with the specific issue of workplace 'bullying' within the schools of the LEA in which the teachers worked. Political action was largely restricted to this level. However, they also sought to influence change nationally in the trade union's policies on 'bullying'.

The two ideologies and aims of the group were evident in group meetings. While much time was spent discussing the political aims of the group and ways to advance them, time was also allocated to the emotional support of members. Many of the group had lost personal and professional confidence and experienced feelings of low self-esteem and sense of worthlessness as a result of their experiences. At the beginning of meetings, members

(approximately twenty members attend each meeting) were asked to introduce themselves and say a little about their experiences of being 'bullied'
at work. In such sessions, members would often refer to themselves as
'victims' or 'targets' of 'bullying' and some talked at length of the trauma
of the experience and its aftermath. The chairperson would invite members
to 'remind each other of the emotions they had experienced'. Members
would respond by 'confirming shared experiences' (Taylor, 1998) and
offering advice to each other. All these personal narratives confirmed that
members had suffered at the hands of management, commonly a headteacher. Many members were 'angry' and sought 'vengeance' against their
'bullies' and unions. This powerful emotional investment in the group and
its self-reflexive project and political aims made the 'personal' genuinely
'political'.

Apart from emotional damage, many of the members had also been financially disadvantaged by being forced to leave teaching before retirement
age, through redundancy procedures or illness retirement. These sought
knowledge of political and legal ways in which they could gain some financial compensation; through monetary awards granted by an employment
tribunal, for instance. In this respect, their values were 'materialist'. They
also sought to remove constraints and oppression on not only their members,
but other workers in the local authority, and in other occupations. Even
with their restricted and localised political ideology and the centring of
their grievances around the economic and the workplace, the group had
emancipatory intentions, at least in terms of Giddens' (1991: 210) definition of emancipatory politics, which is:

> A generic outlook concerned above all with liberating individuals and
> groups from constraints which adversely affect their life chances.
> Emancipatory politics involves two main elements: the effort to shed
> shackles of the past, thereby permitting a transformative attitude
> towards the future; and the aim of overcoming the illegitimate domi-
> nation of some individuals or groups by others.

The group was also involved in 'lifestyle' and 'identity politics'. As Giddens
(1991: 228) argues, 'all questions of life politics raise problems of an emancipatory sort'. In attempting to resolve these problems, the teacher self-help
group had necessarily combined their 'power' and 'identity' orientations
(Rucht, 1990).

Participants

The teacher self-help group was predominantly composed of teachers, but
also included workers from other 'caring' professions (for example, social
workers). All members were white, of a similar age (i.e. mid to late career)
and had similar salaries and lifestyles. There were equal numbers of men

and women. They were a community of 'likeminded individuals who have undergone similar political socialization, follow a similar lifestyle, and show similar problem sensibility' (Brand, 1990: 27).

Ozga and Lawn (1981) argue that the social class location of teachers in the English education system is notoriously difficult to determine. Because they are employed by the state and not, therefore, directly by capital and are engaged in a form of non-productive labour which does not directly generate surplus value they are viewed, by some, to occupy an apparently ambiguous position (neither capital nor labour) between the working class and the state.

All the members of the teacher self-help group were or had been members of trade unions. The founder members, who were subsequently elected as officers of the group, were all members of the largest teacher union, with its roots in the labour movement of the mid-nineteenth century, one fraction of which was noted for militant action on a national scale. These members had been, and in some cases still were, local officials of their union (with whom they were in dispute) and some were active in emancipatory labour movement politics.

The group members, therefore, conformed to many of the characteristics of the 'new radical middle class'. Indeed, some leading group members had strong labour movement credentials. All new social movement members join because they have a 'problem' to solve. In the case of the teacher self-help group, the problem, like Kriesi et al.'s (1995) new middle class workers, was located firmly in issues concerned with the control of work and relationships between managers and workers – the very same issues that have always been of concern to the labour movement.

Structure

The teachers' self-help group began informally with a loose network of 'bullied' teachers who were in contact with each other through union activity. One of the founding members was responsible for contacting people by telephone and letter to inform them of informal meetings in a pub which were held monthly. Once numbers increased the group moved from informality and spontaneity into a phase of 'organisational formalisation' (Offe, 1990). Monthly meetings were held in a hall for which rent had to be paid. A constitution was written and officers (chair, secretary, treasurer) were elected. The chair and secretary were also local union officials. This created a hierarchy in the group and, as Offe (1990) notes, organisational formalisation can cause as many problems as it solves. The group had recorded in their constitution the dangers that creating such a hierarchical structure could recreate the conditions for 'bullying' to take place. Issues were voted on but some decisions were taken unilaterally by a 'committee' without consulting members. This was said to be necessary for reasons of flexibility and rapid decision-making. Debates took place surrounding definitions of 'in' and 'out' group individuals. There was an initial discussion about creating two forms of membership: 'members' who had experienced 'bullying' and, therefore, could be considered as 'victims'; and 'associate members' who had not experienced bullying but were partners of members or were bringing some form of expertise to the group. Lengthy discussions took place about whether to become a limited company or try to achieve charity status. Both options would, it was argued, give some form of limitation of financial liability if any member or the group was sued because of its activities concerned with exposing 'bullies' and 'bullying'. A group name, the acronym of which was a metaphor of the concept 'marginality', was devised and designs for a logo and headed notepaper were put in hand. The group formed a loose federation with other similar groups nationally by inviting speakers to address members at the monthly meetings. Trade unions with which the group was in dispute were approached for financial help. Officers from some of these unions were invited to attend meetings. Discussions at monthly meetings typically would be led by the chair and involved debates about the objectives of the group and progress made in meeting them. We were reminded each time that 'much had been achieved already but much remains to be done' (Offe, 1990: 240).

Great effort went into the maintenance of the group; strategies for attracting new members were discussed; and there were frequent exhortations to pay dues (Offe, 1990) such as the annual fee, collection for monthly room rent and costs for teas and coffees, in order to keep the group financially viable. Members not in work and suffering from financial hardship were not obliged to pay.

Thus, the self-help group adopted a very formal, hierarchical and bureaucratised form of organisation. This was, of course, very similar to the institutions in which they had worked (and had experienced 'bullying'), and to the organisation of the unions with which they were in dispute. This, then, clearly was not a 'new' mode of structure.

Strategies

In terms of 'power' orientation, Dalton and Kuechler (1990: 14) suggest that new social movements have developed 'unconventional political tactics' and seek to achieve their goals through exerting 'political pressure and public opinion' rather than through involvement in 'traditional political structures'. Activity tends to be local with members 'agitating for changes' (Taylor, 1998) by using 'persuasion and bargaining tactics', and attempting to bring reform through such processes as 'public hearings and enquiries' (Rucht, 1990: 159). By contrast, 'identity' oriented strategies are not aimed at changing society but concerned with personal and lifestyle change (Pichardo, 1997). Members engage with the task of beginning to 'build a different life on the basis of an oppressed identity' (Castells, 1997: 9). Such strategies would include consciousness raising and therapeutic activities.

These strategies coincide with the twin aims of our teacher self-help group. The group conducted research amongst its members to survey the incidence and nature of bullying in the LEA schools. They secured a meeting with the CEO and head of personnel in order to 'confront' them with their evidence and agitate for change within the schools of the LEA. As a result of this action representatives of the group were invited on to a working party in order to devise policy on 'bullying' in the LEA. Members used a trade union newsletter in order to circulate information about the group to a wide range of teachers locally. Letters were written to, and published in, the local and national press. Some members appeared on a national television 'chat' show which focused on the theme of bullying in the workplace. One member played a prominent part in a televised documentary on 'bullying' and stress. This member is also a national figure in the anti-bullying movement and had published a book on his personal experience as a victim of bullying in the workplace. He also runs a telephone helpline for victims and a website on which he publicises details of the group globally. This member was the source of much advice on anti-bullying 'repertoires of action' and was consulted frequently by individual members and the group in meetings. Talks were given by 'advocates' who had experience of representing victims of harassment in industrial tribunals and solicitors specialising in employment and personal injury law.

In addition to the affective strategies mentioned earlier, the group engaged in several other self-reflexive activities. Social events, involving meals and visits, were organised at strategic times of the year when members might be feeling 'low'. Links were made with 'conventional' medical services in the local authority; these including 'counselling' facilities. A number of members engaged in bibliotherapy by reading books on case histories of bullying (like the one produced and published by the group member mentioned above) and diagnostic and self-help texts on stress. Discussions took place on a range of 'therapies' and how they could benefit members. Sessions were planned around themes such as: yoga; aromatherapy; 'alternative medicines'; and cognitive therapy. The teacher self-help group, in combining 'power' and 'identity' orientations, was clearly adopting new social movement strategies to progress their aims.

Conclusion

Stressed teachers have been alienated, marginalised, destabilised, disoriented, dehumanised, and disempowered, in our cases after many years of successful teaching. It is not easy to recover from such a state. There are no simple solutions. As we have seen, the task is to re-empower the self, to feel human and like a person again, and to re-enter social life on equal terms. It is difficult to do this on one's own. The teachers themselves have considerable personal resources, but sometimes these have to be stirred or prompted and encouraged by others. They gather strength from others in this way, for example through emotional support from family, or some structured professional association as with a doctor or counsellor, or through some chance occurrence, like a meeting with a former pupil, or experimenting with a new activity. At those levels, however, while the individual teacher might find some relief, the source of the stress is not being tackled. It is at those levels, and especially at the individual level, that previous work on teacher coping strategies has concentrated – 'self' being seen as the main component. With the growth of constraint in recent years, however, there comes a point where the self has to be invested in the group if coping is to succeed. There would appear to be potential in that respect in the self-help group, linked as it is with other occupations, and addressing a general, society-wide problem. There is a certain amount that teachers can do to help themselves individually, and even more when drawing strength from others, but they can do far more operating collectively in this way. If the solution to the escalating rates of teacher stress is not forthcoming from government and/or institutional policy, then the generation of a new social movement seems indicated in order to bring solace to teachers, and to force the pace and focus the minds of the policy makers.

6 Trusting in teamwork
The low-stress school

> The collaborative leadership of change requires a willingness to experiment
> with different ideas and feelings, a team player mentality, a sharing of tasks
> between and among members, and a view of confronting conflict as an
> opportunity for learning and enhancing effectiveness.
>
> (Argyris, 1970, in Diamond, *The Unconscious*
> *Life of Organizations*, 1993: 226)

Introduction

Much of the early research on teacher stress emphasised the importance of
personal psychological factors and task characteristics in the generation of
job-related stress (for a review, see Kyriacou, 1980b). This approach tended
to underestimate the negative effects of school organisation and teacher
culture. More recently, work using a psychological perspective has included
consideration of the organisational structure and social processes within it
as sources of stressors in teachers' work (Travers and Cooper, 1996). From
a sociological perspective, Woods et al. (1997) argue that teacher stress is
a multifaceted and multidimensional phenomenon. While educational
policy and the intensification of work may be 'creating the pressures that
lie behind the rising incidence of stress, organisational structure can affect
how those pressures are played out' (ibid.: 161). Hargreaves (1998a: 316)
writing on the centrality of teachers' emotions in their work sees:

> The emotional lives of educators not only as matters of personal dispo-
> sition or commitment, as psychological qualities that emerge among
> individuals, but also as phenomena that are shaped by how the work
> of teaching is organised, structured and led.

Rosenholtz (1989) focuses on the importance of school organisation and
teacher culture in the generation of stress in beginning teachers. Leithwood
et al. (1999: 112), in their substantial statistical review of quantitative
studies on leadership and organisational factors which contribute to teacher
stress, conclude that:

In the light of evidence indicating that the total effects of this construct (*i.e. organisational factors*) were almost twice as strong as the effects of other constructs (*e.g. personal factors and leadership factors*), this is part of the explanation of variation in teacher burnout critically in need of further work. (*our italics*)

Dinham and Scott (1996: 30), in a large-scale survey of teachers' job satisfaction, motivation and health, also discovered a range of significant school-based factors such as 'school leadership and decision making, school reputation, school climate and school infrastructure', and it is here that 'there is thus greatest potential for change within schools'. Smylie (1999) also emphasises conditions of work in school organisations which are potential and actual factors associated with stress. He argues that role overload, role ambiguity and role conflict are particularly influential in this respect.

Friedman (1991) compared the characteristics and cultures of a large number of high- and low-burnout schools and found that managers in high-burnout schools tended to have an autocratic management style, and measurable goals stressing academic achievement were set. Administrative structures had clearly defined hierarchies with teachers not generally operating in teams. The physical environment of such schools was generally clean and orderly. By contrast, in low-burnout schools educational objectives were flexible with little pressure for high standards. The organisational structure was generally flexible, teachers held meetings in large groups and socialising among teachers in the same school occurred more often in low-burnout than in high burnout schools. The physical environment of low-burnout schools was not especially clean and tidy. An overall finding was that 'hard-driving school policy induces strong stress that is conducive to teacher burnout' (ibid.: 331). The 'tight ship' approach advocated by Rutter et al. (1979), while presumably increasing educational achievement, apparently might do so at the expense of teachers' physical and mental health.

In this chapter, we examine some aspects of a 'low-stress' school in order to reveal features of 'organizational design that minimize members chances of experiencing burnout' (Leithwood et al., 1999: 12). D. Hargreaves (1994) has argued that teachers' occupational cultures are currently in transition with a shift taking place from individualism and isolation to teamworking and collaboration. We need to know the positive and negative consequences of these changes for teachers' work (Smyth, 1991). Also, a case study which involves 'studying teachers and conditions of teaching where higher levels of emotional understanding are being achieved can give us valuable insights and clues as to how to reform teaching more widely' (Hargreaves, 1998c: 840).

The case study school and research methods

Stanhope Road was described by Ofsted as a 'sound school with many strengths in its teaching staff. . . . Pupils are well integrated and there is a positive ethos which recognises children as individuals'. The inspection report stated that:

> The school is part of the LEA's cluster provision for children with moderate learning difficulties and is linked to a special school. In the main, it serves its local community with most of its pupils living in the immediate area. The school admits pupils at the beginning of the year following their fourth birthday. Its intake represents a cross section of the community in socio-economic terms and covers the normal ability range. Most pupils have had pre-school education and about 80 per cent are ready to learn. 1.6 per cent of pupils have a statement of SEN which is slightly above the county average. However fewer pupils in the school are being statemented and this is an indicator of the success the school is having in providing for pupils with SEN rather than the result of a variation in policy. Overall 23 per cent of pupils are on the school's SEN register and receive extra help. The proportion of pupils receiving free school meals is 15.3 per cent which is similar to the national average. Approximately 11 per cent of pupils are of ethnic minority backgrounds, again similar to the national average. No pupils are in need of Section 11 support for English as an additional language.

The headteacher, Keith Roberts, described the school as follows:

> The school has a very, very mixed catchment area. We've got very expensive Victorian houses. But there's also a lot of multi-occupied private rented accommodation in this area. We take a lot of our kids, 70 per cent plus from out of the area. And they tend to be not quite deprived wards but certainly less affluent than this ward. We've got about 5 per cent Asian children mainly from India. They're third or fourth generation. So we don't have to teach English as a second language but we have to be aware that sometimes their language is a bit stilted and sometimes slightly less good than some of the other children because of the background at home where the parents are often speaking Gujarati or Punjabi.

Some characteristics of the pupils can be seen from the pupil data shown in Table 6.1. Teachers and classes are shown in Table 6.2.

Stanhope Road Primary was a self-defined 'low-stress' school which had recently received a highly favourable Ofsted report and had low teacher absence rates, low staff sickness rates, low staff turnover, and high

Table 6.1 Pupil data – Stanhope Road Primary School

	Number of pupils on roll (full-time equivalent)	Number of pupils with statements of SEN	Number of pupils on school's register of SEN	Number of full-time pupils eligible for free school meals
YR–Y6	307	5	71	47 (15.3%)

Table 6.2 Teachers and classes – Stanhope Road Primary School

Qualified teachers (YR–Y6)	
Total number of qualified teachers	11.4
Number of pupils per qualified teacher	27
Average class size	31

Table 6.3 Details of teachers – Stanhope Road Primary School

Name	Age	Key stage	Post
Keith	52	1 & 2	Headteacher
Alison	40	1	English Co-ordinator
Stephanie	48	1	Science Co-ordinator
Louise	23	2	Newly Qualified Teacher
Imogen	48	2	Art Co-ordinator
Caroline	30	1	KS 1 Co-ordinator
Doreen	50	2	IT Co-ordinator
Maria	35	1	Music Co-ordinator
Lynn	50	2	RE Co-ordinator
Bryony	52	1 & 2	SEN Teacher
Tricia	55	2	Humanities Co-ordinator
Kate	54	2	KS 2 Co-ordinator
Andrea	50	2	Maths Co-ordinator

teacher morale. This school had been approached because of an article written by the headteacher on the prevention of stress in schools. He saw stress prevention/alleviation as a prime responsibility of management. He was also keen to have the teachers involved in the research and did much to enlist their support. Keith told us, 'Out of the 11.4 teachers, three are in their thirties, or below, and the rest are forty plus. So there's a skew – and they're all women. I'm the only man.' Staff turnover was low, with the majority of teachers having taught there for a number of years, and sickness rates and absences did not give cause for concern.

The headteacher was interviewed as part of a preliminary day visit to the school in June 1998. Early the following term, Geoff spent three days in the school observing social interactions in the staffroom, shared teaching areas and corridors and conducting interviews with teachers and some support staff. In all, thirteen semi-structured interviews of about one hour's duration each were carried out. Details of the teachers interviewed are shown in Table 6.3.

Trusting in teamwork

The organisation and culture of teaching which contributed to the low incidence of stress at the school were characterised by *Trust*, *Openness*, *Sharing*, *Supporting*, *Understanding* and *Realism*.

Trust

The discourse and practice of teamwork was a salient feature of Stanhope Road Primary. It had invested trust in teamwork as a mode of organisation which would enable the school to run 'efficiently' and 'effectively' while preventing high levels of stress in the governors, headteacher, teachers and ancillary staff. Teamwork in this context revealed high levels of trust between team members. Bryony said, 'You have to trust somebody. I have to trust that the pupils are there, the staff are there and somehow we're going to work that out.' Keith said, 'I think people trust each other so if they say they're going to get a job done they'll actually do it.' Louise, an NQT, considered that, owing to the relationship she had with colleagues, she had 'really landed on her feet getting a job here'. Although there was no 'whole-school' collaborative culture (Nias et al., 1989) owing to a physical separation of infant and junior departments, there were a number of teams whose membership changed periodically. For instance, there were KS teams, year teams, and teams for policy making, planning and teaching. There was a strong sense of 'togetherness' (see Chapter 1) in the school. Kate, a senior teacher, talked of 'team spirit' and there was a feeling of 'all being in it together' and 'all being in the same boat' (Caroline). Caroline felt that teamwork had been partly stimulated by their Ofsted inspection:

> One of the good things that came out of the Ofsted inspection was that everybody did pull together and everybody felt exactly the same. So it did actually pull people together as a team.

She thought the teamwork ethos had its origins in the reception department where she taught:

> I then moved into a building with another teacher so we had two reception classes. We had probably the closest working team within the school. We actually got on very well and started off the original shared grievances, shared celebrations and patting each other on the back for certain things and actually building up each other's strengths when the other was low.

Kate said:

> We try to support each other and work in teams ... I've worked in schools where you go into a classroom, close the door and you're on your own. Everything's been left up to you to do. You are isolated – nobody's interested in what you're doing and you're not interested in what anybody else is doing, whereas here we actually work in teams, such as, planning teams. We swap with each other, we swap classes for different things and you don't get this feeling of being alone. I think you feel that people are interested in what you're doing, because what you're doing impacts on what they're doing as well. And you're not just left to struggle.

Keith was very clear that although personal factors are involved in stress the institution can generate it, so the mode of organization and type of staff relationships are crucial in prevention:

> I think it's really important that people work in an atmosphere where they feel pleasantly assured that they can get on with their job and no-one's hassling them and that they're not feeling frustrated. I think teachers feel frustrated enough anyway without having the sort of institution they work for causing them to feel more frustrated. I don't think it's just people – individuals. I think there is something about personality and kinds of person that get probably more stressed than others. But I think it's the institution as well that can create atmospheres and situations where people can't do the job properly.

His solution lay in trusting teamwork:

> We always work in teams so there's hardly anybody has to feel they have to take a massive decision that causes them to go home and worry about it or spend a lot of time round the school getting fractious about it and thinking, 'What am I going to do?'

Openness

Beatty (1999: 22), writing about teacher development and emotional cultures of teaching, argues that:

> It is possible that a culture of emotional restraint where 'never is heard a disparaging word' may be costing organizations like schools the opportunity to engage in honest critique and self-evaluation, both important dimensions of organizational learning and responsiveness.

In some schools where teachers do engage in critique, it is more in a spirit of conflict and competition rather than mutual development (Ball, 1987). In some of our research (Troman, 1997; Woods et al., 1997; Jeffrey and Woods, 1998), we have found stressful situations being created (commonly between teachers and headteachers) by 'closed' relationships involving poor or no communication, withdrawn and/or incompetent leadership, and head-teachers engaging in micro-political strategies.

By contrast, staff relationships at Stanhope Road were characterised by the type of openness found in some families. This mode of relationship seemed to pertain in Alison's family where:

> Seven o'clock is family meal time. And we're all home and everybody will sort of sit down and thrash the day out then.

Keith felt that principles of openness underpinned the organisation of the school:

> I've got an open style of management, I hope. Nothing's closed. Nothing's secret. Everything's up for grabs. So if there are jobs going and posts going it's public, and people have to bear in mind that if two people apply for it, one's going to be disappointed.

Approachability

Kate recalled working in institutions which were 'closed' and where teachers were inhibited from approaching colleagues on professional issues, and this led to counter-productive isolationism:

> I have worked in schools where it seems a weakness to say you're having a problem with something, or to admit that you weren't *au fait* with what you were teaching or whatever. And you kept it quiet and just went off on your own trying to find books to gen up on it.

Louise also, in other schools, had not always found it easy to approach colleagues for help because she recognised they were also very busy, and she did not wish to be a 'pest'.

Dealing with 'difficult' pupils was a potential source of stress in the teachers' work (see also Rosenholtz, 1989; Woods et al., 1997; Hargreaves, 1998a) While pupils provide many of the psychic rewards of teaching (Lortie, 1975), they can also generate some 'annoyances' (Hargreaves, 1999b). Keith felt that he could now be approached by teachers who were experiencing difficulties with their classes but this had not always been the case:

We haven't had any difficulties with teachers admitting that they can't deal with individuals. . . . But I think we've had some difficult classes in the past that we've had teachers struggling with, really difficult classes because the combination of kids in it has been really, really difficult to teach. . . . We've had teachers there that have been frightened to admit that actually the whole class is getting them down.

Doreen, who had 'battled on alone' in the past, found Keith 'very easy to talk to', and it was 'better to talk than to bottle things up'. Alison also found that she could 'go and talk to' Keith and the governors also were 'great'. As one of the three teachers who collectively fulfilled the deputy headteacher role, Kate was keen to make herself accessible, both directly and as an intermediary between a member of staff and the headteacher, because sometimes people were reluctant to approach him because 'they don't want to appear like a whinger'. Maria felt able to approach anyone on the staff on professional matters without experiencing embarrassment. 'There were some lovely, lovely teachers on the staff here, and I know I could go to any of them if I had any problems or queries or if I didn't know how to teach a particular lesson.'

The nature, pace and uncertainties of policy changes were stimulating openness and approachability in the school. The implementation of the literacy hour, for example, was 'really showing that people aren't afraid to say, "I don't know what to do". "What are we doing?"'

Keith was aware of the consequences of not being open and approachable on matters of organisation. This was owing to the occasional lapse in communication on his part. On one occasion he had forgotten to tell people that the school secretary was going with a school party to Jersey, and 'the person that's going to be left behind looking after everyone was quite cross about this'.

The school had introduced an induction system involving mentoring which included new teachers to the school 'so that they don't feel isolated and they can ask what they might feel are stupid questions like: Where's the art cupboard? Where's the projector? Am I allowed to photocopy?' There was also a 'pairing' system where teachers met regularly together to discuss any professional or personal issues they wished. They could 'sit down and thrash out any problems and tell each other all the snags or issues or problems that they're having in that subject'.

Honesty

A great deal of research on schools and classrooms shows a large amount of strategic work among teachers as they seek to gain their ends in competition with others and/or with limited resources (Blase, 1991; Blase and Anderson, 1995). Much of this might be micro-political activity (Ball, 1987). There are also 'presentation of fronts' and playing to situations

(Goffman, 1959). In many of these instances, there is a suggestion of subterfuge if not duplicity. Stanhope Road seemed notable for its honesty. Keith felt he was honest in his relationships with the teachers:

> One of the teachers once praised me by saying it was really good that if you say you're going to do something you actually do it. And I do do it, I think. And if I can't, I'll say I can't. And if I say I'm going to do it and then I can't, and I suddenly think, 'Oh I promised to do that but I can't now', I'll say that as well – be honest. I'll go and teach, if somebody wants some time out. But I'm very honest in saying no. I'm not willing to go and teach if I'll just do it badly, because someone's asked me suddenly. I'll say, 'I'll consider it but I'll need some notice so that I can do it properly.' Or if I do have to do it in two minutes, I'll make it clear it'll be lousy because I haven't prepared anything.

Lynn felt able to be honest with the headteacher in an assertive way, by being able to, 'say no to Keith without agonising too much'. Kate had adopted an honest and open approach to her preparation for the Ofsted inspection:

> All the things I did I didn't want them to be window dressing. I wanted them to take us as we were. But I wanted to make sure that I got everything right in my classroom or around the school . . . I didn't want us just to do safe things. I wanted them to see what we actually do. And if there is a problem with it, let us know about it. There was no point in papering over any cracks or hiding anything from them. I thought the school ought to function as it normally does – warts and all.

Doreen recalls an occasion when she felt she could not admit difficulties she was having with her class; these later proved stressful:

> I had actually offered to take this class. It was bigger than average and had thirty-six children because that was the whole year group. Before that I'd been taking mainly year six. And when we were trying to sort out the classes it was going to be awkward. I don't think it's ever a good idea to have just one or two children of an age group completely with another age group. So I had actually offered to take this class as a whole class. You know, I was to get some extra support because of it, but then when I did find the going a bit difficult – I think it was a matter of pride that I'd sort of dug myself into that hole and didn't want to admit that I was actually finding it a bit more difficult than I had thought. But when I think back over it, it was the combination of children, that it wasn't an easy class.

Sharing

Democratic participation has been shown to be an efficacious form of teacher culture (Nias et al., 1989). This might be contrasted with the hierarchical nature of managerialism. As we have seen in Chapters 2 (high stress) and 3 (bullying), the production of teacher stress currently has strong associations with the latter. Unsurprisingly, perhaps, Stanhope Road favoured the former arrangement, practising it on a broad basis. The teachers shared values, knowledge and expertise, responsibilities, resources and a sense of humour.

Values

Hargreaves (1998a: 322) argues that 'the emotions of teaching, their nature and form are . . . shaped by the moral purposes of those who teach'. When these purposes are in conflict with those of colleagues, 'anxiety, frustration, anger and guilt affect everyone who is involved' and teachers might 'lose energy and enthusiasm for their work' (Hargreaves, 1999a: 21).

With regard to Stanhope Road, Ofsted reported that, 'The school's aims place emphasis on tolerance and mutual co-operation and these values are successfully promoted throughout the school.' As in other effective schools (Nias et al., 1989), these shared values prioritised human relationships.

Lynn now finds she has common values with her job share partner:

> The job share that I'm in now is far less stressful than when I job shared with somebody previously. . . . There were two very different outlooks on everything, and that was more difficult.

One teacher was aware of the negative consequences of working in a previous school where values were not shared:

> I was ill with stress . . . a lot of it was not feeling valued. The head that I worked for at that time was a very autocratic person who actually had got clear ideas about how his school should be and how the children should be. And my argument was that the children we'd got needed a different regime from the one that we were trying to operate. And that wasn't accepted at all. I felt my head was trying to run a middle class establishment in a quite deprived working class area . . . we should have been more flexible in the way that we dealt with pupils and the way that we addressed issues. And I was a co-ordinator there so I was a senior member of staff. I worked there before he came and my and his views were opposite, for instance he introduced these Richmond tests which are a bit like the SATs but worse in my view. And I had children who were traveller children in my class and I knew very well that the test booklet would have been an absolute mystery.

I said, 'Does Kerry have to do this?' And he said, 'Yes'. And I said, 'Why?' Afterwards he said, 'Don't question me ... Because she's got to learn'. And, of course, I said, 'To learn she can't do it?' And then he said I was being insubordinate. And it was that kind of conflict all the time. Like he spent three weeks testing every child in the school on that reading test, which I felt was an absolute waste of a head-teacher's time. And it was that sort of philosophical conflict that we had. And I couldn't actually operate within that system without selling out my principles – I had to find a way of coping with it.

Knowledge and expertise

Stanhope Road showed many of the features of a learning community (Retallick et al., 1999). For example, there was much sharing of knowledge and expertise in the school. All found they could learn from somebody else whatever their role or status (Woods, 1999b). Keith said that:

> I ask the caretaker's advice and other people do. I think it sort of rubs off on other people in a way. My secretary's an expert on IT. I can't use her computer. I'm quite willing to admit that to anyone. I couldn't do what she does.

Sharing of knowledge and expertise took place in formal and informal processes. Keith reported:

> They do feel valued by each other, because they tell each other that we're doing a good job and what's good. And we try and use each other's expertise. If we've got someone who's very good at getting some very good art work out of kids, we try and find out from her how she does it so that we can all do it. It's that sort of shared expertise and shared values. Somebody who's very good at PE and people are always saying, 'How do you do that – make the kids do that? Because they'll never do it when I want them to do it'. So we share.

The type of person who thrived in this type of organisation was a problem solver who could rely on the skills and knowledge of others when tackling the problems that arose. The kind of people Keith tries to recruit are

> problem solvers rather than people who say, 'Oh God, we've got a problem, we've got a problem, we've got a problem', and just moan about it. So if problems do crop up, I think almost – the ones recently – almost every single time it's been, 'Let's – come on what are we doing to solve it'. Not, 'Oh let's panic' ... You know that realistically every week in a school of this size there's going to be some kind of problem that needs solving, maybe one person can just crack it easily, or maybe

two or three people need to get their heads together, or maybe it's a big problem and we need to take months working out a different policy.

Sharing problems and seeking collective solutions using shared expertise were applied to one of the teachers' main professional concerns – 'difficult' pupils:

> KEITH: Everyone knows they're difficult. So no one expects any one indi-
> vidual to find a solution. They just try different techniques. So some-
> times I'll have a go and get something good out of them and sometimes
> it's obvious I'm not doing very well with them and somebody else will
> try. So again it's knowing. I think if the teacher's isolated in the class-
> room with a kid like that, and day after day they're banging their head
> on a brick wall and whatever they try is not working, I think that
> would be very stressful. And that shouldn't be allowed to happen.
> Somebody ought to be there on hand to work something different out
> for them. . . . . It's part of our behaviour policy that if certain children
> are causing problems in the classroom, try somebody else. . . . So it's a
> shared knowledge that these kids are difficult, and nobody should be
> expected to deal with them on their own.

Kate benefited from sharing the curricular and pedagogic knowledge of colleagues in informal staffroom discussions:

> I say to myself, 'I'm glad I haven't got to do this on my own.' I ask
> the others, 'What are you doing in this lesson?' It's just little ideas they
> give you. They say, 'I've done this with my class, but perhaps you can
> do it at a higher level or a lower level. You can adapt things.' So it's
> a source of ideas.

Louise shares with teachers and LSAs:

> We talk about the children and we share ideas on classroom manage-
> ment and how to get the most out of them and share work that we're
> doing with our classes, so we can adapt it for our children. That's really
> helpful.

Keith explained that the 'pairing' system (described by Maria as a 'sharing shop') formalises and complements the informal sharing system:

> Originally it was designed just so that they'd got someone else to bounce
> ideas off and someone else to take the pressure off if they were feeling
> frazzled about having to do something. Somebody else might say, 'Well,
> if you do it this way it's probably easier', or 'Yes, I can see you've got
> a problem. Let's try and sit and work it out'. So it wasn't done just to

try and spread the expertise. It was done also to solve problems that might crop up.

The skills of the governors, most of them in professional occupations, were utilised in organisational processes and shared with the teachers. Keith described them as 'an absolutely brilliant group of governors'.

Bryony shared her knowledge of stress and coping with teachers at Stanhope Road and at other schools in in-service training sessions:

> I run courses and I have to be very careful when I'm talking to teachers because I say things like, 'I try not to take work home'. I would sooner stay here till six o'clock or seven o'clock or, like last night, nine o'clock, and finish it and walk out because the biggest stress maker I've found is the 'bag in the hall'. This is the bag of school work you took home with you and that you find in the morning, unopened because of tiredness and domestic pressures, which puts you in a rotten frame of mind because you've failed before you've even gone out of the front door.

Responsibilities

There was no clear hierarchy in the school. Roles and responsibilities were, as in the problem solving example, often interchangeable. Keith, for example, on occasions, would fulfil the caretaker's responsibilities, unlocking and locking up when he had a few days' holiday. Bryony felt 'most comfortable in schools where I feel I own decisions that have been made. I feel I've contributed to it.' But Keith was sometimes reminded of his responsibilities by his staff. They told him to 'Go away and do the targets' one day when they were 'fed up of talking about them'. The democratic consensus did not run to doing the headteacher's work for him!

Resources

The teachers shared resources for their lessons. Kath told us:

> Nobody keeps their resources to themselves. It's not that sort of school where you've got your stuff in your classroom and it stays there. We've got a resource centre if you can call it that, and everything's in there and people just go and help themselves.

There did not seem to be a history of repeated budget cuts in the school. This positive financial situation made it possible for subject co-ordinators to 'bid' for funds in order to 'buy' themselves out of the classroom in order to complete administrative tasks. Without this shared resource the work would have had to be completed in school after the school day or at the co-ordinator's home in the evening or at the weekend. The school's favourable financial position allowed generous levels of classroom support from LSAs, which were shared equitably throughout the school.

Humour

The capacity of humour to rehumanise situations and to enable coping and survival in schools is well known (Woods, 1990; Dubberley, 1993; Jeffrey and Woods, 1998). Its absence is an indication of problems (Jeffrey and Woods, 1995). Stanhope Road was notable for its shared humour.

> They're usually hooting with laughter about something in the staff room. A lot of laughter in the kids as well. . . . And the children are quite relaxed about life. The teachers are quite relaxed enough to laugh along. They find quite a lot of amusing things out of the school day – during the school day, not just after the day's finished when they're probably just relaxing for half an hour before they do some paperwork. Yes, it is important. . . . To have good fun.

Observation of social interactions in the staffroom and around the school supported the headteacher's testimony. The 'pairing' scheme was a social process in which laughter played a key part.

> KEITH: The person who was the NQT actually appreciated that they could have a good laugh with the other person sometimes, as well as it being a sort of professional context.

Caroline thought her:

> sense of humour had developed more over the years. Towards the beginning you tend to hold back a little bit of yourself, but then when you start to realise that this school is your life then you settle more with it. And we certainly have a laugh. We don't get too bogged down by things. We take things at quite a nice pace, but we also get on with the nitty gritty and say things that need saying. With the people I work directly with it's almost as though we don't have to say certain things. We've worked together as a team for so long that they can almost read my mind.

There are echoes here of the headteacher and deputy in Nias (1987) research who worked so closely together they were 'like finger like thumb'. Even the Ofsted team who carried out their inspection blended in with the school in this respect, making it a less traumatic experience than other schools have found (Jeffrey and Woods, 1998):

KATE: They weren't stand-offish. . . . You'd walk in the school in the morning and they'd say, 'Hi Kate' and they knew your name. . . . They'd have a laugh with you after. I didn't feel as though they were like that when they were actually watching me and writing and scribbling away but I must say whenever I came across them they were friendly and they were human.

Supporting

> Collaborative cultures support and affirm the teacher ... teachers who know their leaders care about and support them in shared values, and moral purposes seem to thrive – emotionally, intellectually and spiritually.
>
> (Beatty, 1999: 3)

Teachers who are trusted and supported by colleagues are willing to take risks in improving their teaching, but when mistrust prevails they are 'inclined to play safe' (Hargreaves, 1998a: 319). In Beatty's (1999: 24) research, 'trust and safety were associated with supportive encouraging leadership, while suspicion and fear were paired with restrictive and controlling administrators'. And the teachers favoured a workplace which was a 'fair and just place, where what teachers say is listened to and teachers' well-being is cared about'.

Bryony, an SEN support teacher, preferred the 'naturally' supportive primary school teacher culture to the 'balkanised' (Hargreaves, 1994) secondary one:

> I think teachers are naturally supportive, particularly in primary schools. I don't think it's quite the same in secondaries because they're so fragmented and they have their own huge faculties and there's a lot more politics in secondary schools and I don't like working in secondary schools much.

Tricia, formerly a supply teacher but now on temporary contract, 'dreaded going back on the road again' as a supply because of the support to which she had become accustomed at the school.

Bryony had engaged in professional learning while supporting others. She was 'always dancing to someone else's tune, always following', but on the other hand, she was 'always encouraging, always supporting'. Kate found that support from colleagues prevented her self-esteem, confidence and sense of efficacy from being undermined as it had been done in other school contexts. People in the past had made her feel 'as though you weren't coping, you weren't doing the meeting very well'. But she never felt that now. People were very supportive in meetings:

I think the people who are here appreciate that we're all in it together and nobody's an expert and we're all trying to do our best. I don't feel as though anybody's going to be out to catch me out or try and make me feel small, or that I don't know what I'm talking about.

During the Ofsted inspection week the staff offered each other structured emotional support. Those with lower grades had been angry, but 'we always made sure there was somebody in the staff room at the end of the day so that anybody who was upset could come in and just sound off and we would listen and try and support'.

Many of the teachers gained a sense of security from receiving 'back-up' from colleagues (Beatty, 1999), especially from Keith, when they experienced difficulties with pupils and parents. Doreen had 'spoken to parents with him', and she thought 'he's been on the whole very supportive of what I've been trying to do or my reasons for acting in a particular way'. On one occasion Keith intervened in a violent classroom incident in order to remove a pupil who 'had to be shut in the library because he was trying to kick and bite Keith and he was calling him everything under the sun'. Kate sought and received Keith's help when she considered that the Ofsted inspectors were observing too many of her lessons. They were making her 'extremely nervous'. She had told Keith, 'I've had somebody on my back for the last two days. It's causing me a problem.' And he said, 'Well they're not supposed to be with you so much. I'll have a word with them about it.'

Research indicates that teachers improve their practice and view of themselves as teachers if given regular constructive feedback on their performance (Rosenholtz, 1989; Leithwood et al., 1999). This occurred at Stanhope Road. Lynn found the appraisal system in the school had done this for her. It helped her 'to vocalise problems that I thought I'd got', and 'little things were done to help or push me in the direction that I wanted to go'.

The trusting support of colleagues increased Alison's self-confidence, which transformed her self-image and self-esteem:

Kate was brilliant for confidence giving and Keith's the same. And they've both said, 'You could do anything if you want to do it.' Kate would say something at meetings or I would offer to do something. And she would say, 'Oh yes, I know I don't have to worry about that because you'll be doing it. And she asked me if I'd ever thought of being a deputy head, and I said I'm actually thinking about it now. And she said, 'Oh well you could do the job'. And Keith will say things like, 'Oh that was an excellent English presentation Alison'. And if he gives me something to do I say, 'When do you want me to come back to you with it', and he'll say, 'Well I don't need to give you a date because I know that you'll deliver it. If I've asked you to do it I know you'll do it.' And lots of little things like that. It is that strange mixture of not really thinking that you were capable of doing things but having been told you were, you felt they couldn't be wrong.

Keith was supportive in practical ways when teachers experienced domestic difficulties which impinged on their professional lives and the work of the school. Lynn, a temporary part-time teacher, had found:

> Keith's main help was he never put anything extra in the way and never caused any problem. If I needed any time like when mum was ill, he let me take her to hospital. If it was a day I was working, that wasn't a problem. No, he was very helpful in that way. But he wasn't supportive in listening or asking the right questions. He wasn't supportive in that way but . . .

Many of the teachers reported that they received a great deal of support from their families. In Lynn's case, her partner was perceptive of her emotions and was emotionally supportive:

> If I've had a bad day, and if it's a bad day it's usually a Wednesday because I've stayed all day and sometimes I begrudge having to stay. So I might go home, and if something else has gone wrong at home I really don't want to know. I sometimes take the dog for a walk and it doesn't seem quite so bad when I come back in. Jim will either listen and ask what went wrong or he won't. He'll try and work out if it's one he needs to listen to or not. I suppose he judges my reaction, the way I've gone in and sometimes he'll make me a coffee, sometimes he'll pour me a gin.

Understanding

'Understanding' is a key feature of effective schools. This is a well-known attribute of the effective teacher in pupils' eyes (Docking, 1987), but it is equally important among teachers themselves. They require high levels of emotional understanding (Denzin, 1984), where the 'emotions being displayed are grounded in experiences that people share in common or in close relationships that they have established over time' (Hargreaves, 1998c: 839).

Headteachers need to understand the innovative capacity of teachers in order to avoid 'teachers and leaders trying to push onwards to the next summit before they are physically and psychologically ready' (Hargreaves, 1998a: 325). Without this understanding, these leaders and their schools can 'overreach themselves and move into a state of entropy where teachers become exhausted and disillusioned or leave' (Fink, 1999: 133). Beatty's (1999) teachers enjoyed working for leaders who knew them and understood and were interested in them as human beings.

Others

Bryony, who had considerable experience of working in industry and many other schools, was clear that schools are 'people places' and the best managers understand those that work for them. They were 'good people managers first', even though headteachers were now financial managers – 'which actually doesn't change their quality as managers of people, and schools are people places'.

Alison had received a poor evaluation from Ofsted, but still felt secure within the school in that she knew what she could do, and that 'the staff and Keith know what I can do'. Keith appeared to understand how the staff liked to be approached with tasks. Bryony explained that 'Everybody's asked. And I think that's a big thing. That's how you get the best out of people.' Keith would ask teachers if they would do something rather than telling them to do it. Kate said, 'He wouldn't tell. No. Keith's not a teller. No.' He understood the teachers' capacity for tasks, could set 'reasonable' deadlines and pace the work. He did not 'pressurise us', was 'very kind, very sweet', and you had 'plenty of warning of when things need to be done by'. Alison said that 'the school runs smoothly but there's no sort of whip cracking or anything like that. I don't think there needs to be.' Kate felt Keith had a 'laid back management style'. If you needed more time, he would say, 'Well, okay, I'll give you a couple of more days and that's it'. It could be 'infuriating' at times, but she preferred that way of working to 'heads who do tell you what to do and it's okay if you agree with what they're saying. But if you disagree . . . it is very frustrating.' From Keith's point of view, he 'didn't see any point in being bloody minded about something that's just not possible for a person to physically do it. It's a sort of life to us here in a way isn't it – compromise.'

Alison, the English co-ordinator, understood her own emotional state and that of her colleagues:

> At the moment I'm disseminating the information for the literacy hour and trying to make sure that the staff are feeling comfortable. Because they are all friends I don't want them to feel stressed because of what I am supposed to be getting them to do. And that I find really hard, because I know that when they know it's a staff meeting about literacy or we've got another training day, I can see them, 'Oh no, not more. Not more!'. And it's me who's doing that to them, and I don't particularly like that.

This kind of understanding headed off the kind of consequences in a school studied by Jeffrey and Woods (1999: 126), where 'the pressures on teachers with a managerial role to be 'managers' were undermining the human relationships among the staff that cemented the collaborative culture typical of the school'. Keith brought emotional understanding to parents and to colleagues as people. One of his young teachers had just lost her father, very suddenly; another had been deserted by her husband. He understood how they felt, and was 'always aware that people bring into work what's going on at home'. Parents, too, came to him in a distressed state about 'partners disappearing and being beaten up and so on'. He gave them time and listened to them. He did not actually consider counselling his strong suit, but he had teachers who were 'better at that, and they take it off my shoulders'. Here again, teamwork operates behind the general understanding, the headteacher making the best use of his team's resources.

Self

As well as understanding others, many teachers also understood themselves and their emotions and reactions in stressful situations. Caroline's confidence was given a boost when she found she could cope with the inspection. She had always doubted her ability to 'cope with stress', and wondered if she would be:

> one of those people that would just collapse completely during the summer beforehand. So I was quite pleased with myself that I didn't collapse in a complete heap. I actually had the resilience. So that was self-affirming . . . and after that I thought well if I can manage that, I can manage anything.

Teachers provided many examples of the stressful experiences that the teachers had coped with in the past. Lynn for example explained that she had had a very traumatic three to four years during which she and her husband had split up and both her parents had died. But she had come through it, and 'everything's much more stable now' and she considered 'you've got to come out of it better. You've got to be stronger and I think that helps me cope'.

Realism

A prominent feature of primary teachers' attempts to handle the changes following the introduction of the National Curriculum in 1988 was 'over-conscientiousness' (Campbell and Neill, 1994; Evans et al., 1994). Their attempts to do the impossible in the face of unreasonable requirements led to a sharp increase in stress and illness among them.

At Stanhope Road, teachers had a more realistic approach. They were very pragmatic. Teachers talked of 'getting things done'. Keith would urge 'Okay, let's deal with it. We've got to do it. Let's do it. Let's find a way of doing it', as they did with having to change their thematic cycle every three to four years following changes in the National Curriculum. He felt that, as headteacher, he should be 'realistic about what people can do and how much you can expect people to do'. Louise, when comparing Stanhope Road with other schools, felt it was:

Detailed and firm, but realistic. Whereas sometimes in other schools, yes it's detailed and firm but it's a joke. It's too much. So that obviously makes a difference. So if you've got the right head who knows what's realistic in terms of expectations of somebody, that's great.

Keith felt 'stress came from the top' and had its origins in headteachers' behaviour and expectations (cf. Chapter 3). It often came, he thought, from striving for an unachievable perfection, where 'in some ways you're on a hiding to nothing because you're not going to get there'. These views were echoed by Bryony who recalled the headteacher of another school where she had worked. He had taken 'early retirement because of severe stress. . . . He'd got to have everything perfect – his favourite word was pristine. He wanted his school pristine, whatever that meant. And he worked night and day to have everything perfect. Well you can't do it.' Keith's aim rather was to make teaching 'as effective and efficient as possible so that every kid succeeds. That's a fine aim I think, to be realistic. And you get reasonable SATs results. Our Ofsted report was fine. It doesn't seem to have made us a less good school than others.' Doreen thought 'you just have to do what you can do and sometimes forget the rest . . . there are only so many hours in a day and only so much you can do and if you try to work conscientiously you have to prioritise.'

On the day of his interview for this research Keith told the LEA inspectors that they had set unrealistically high targets for literacy and told them what the school could realistically 'deliver'.

Conclusion

We have identified the major, generative source of the escalating incidence of teacher stress as the particular form of educational restructuring adopted by government in England and Wales. We have seen in Chapters 2 and 3 how the pressures and conflicts resulting from this have been played out at institutional level. In the 'high-stress' school of Chapter 2, the constraints were reinforced by Ofsted, the agency of the system, exerting 'disciplinary power' in Foucault's (1977) terms. We have shown elsewhere (Jeffrey and Woods, 1998) how this can lead to colonisation of teachers' time and space, and to feelings of deprofessionalisation. This happened to the teachers featuring in Chapter 2. They experienced feelings of guilt, shame, and self-doubt and felt themselves to be inadequate, fraudulent and stigmatised. The grading of teachers led to divisiveness among them. Prominent among the coping strategies adopted were leaving teaching, rationalising the situation, and adopting more instrumental commitment – positive in terms of the teachers coping, negative in terms of children's education. In Chapter 3 we saw the consequences of a hierarchical managerial structure, with bullying cascading down through the system, exacerbated by questionable leadership.

The comparison with the teachers featuring in this chapter could not be more marked. Here we have high self-esteem, morale and confidence, all founded on a culture of trust. This enables a genuine collaborative culture (not one 'contrived' in purely managerial interests – see Hargreaves, 1994) to develop, marked by teams operating at different levels – department, pairs. Like the best sports teams, these are not just a collection of individuals – the team is bigger and better than the sum of its parts. Within this environment, individuals can be open and honest with each other, as opposed to being isolated and competitive, using their knowledge, skills and other resources for mutual benefit in a common aim, as opposed to using their best creativity to advance their own individual cause in institutional micro-politics. They do not succumb to rational technocracy, but sustain a high level of emotional understanding about their professional relationships, both among themselves and with their pupils. This is positive rather than the negative use of the emotions that pervades Chapters 2 and 3. Nor do they make the honest mistake of many primary teachers of 'over-conscientiousness', striving for an 'unachievable perfectionism', identified in the early years following the introduction of the National Curriculum as a major factor in teacher stress (Campbell and Neill, 1994). Their drive for quality is no less, and all the more effective for being founded on realistic objectives. This does not mean that they are not adventurous. They can take risks within certain clearly defined areas, supported and cushioned by the team.

Evident, too, is a different use of power. At Stanhope Road there is democratic participation. The principle of equal inputs underwrites the collaborative culture. The headteacher has ultimate authority, but he does not abuse his power, as do the headteachers in Chapter 3. It is invested in the interests of the team, where it serves another purpose in addition to strengthening the bonds within the group. Seen against the external force of government policy, it is helping to generate a form of power consisting of 'relationships of co-operation, mutual support and equity' (Bloome and Willett, 1991: 208). These relationships can prop up and indeed advance the values of the group, which are all the more sharply defined by the comparison with those sought to be imposed from without (see Woods, 1995b, Chapter 3). There are signs here, too, that this form of power is being extended beyond the school in an incipient learning community (Retallick et al., 1999). This is not just a matter of avoiding stress. There is growing evidence of its educational strengths (Fink, 1999). The particular Ofsted team that conducted an inspection of the school supported these developments, and in a sense also became part of the learning community. What this chapter shows, therefore, is that cascading bullying and deprofessionalisation is not an inevitable consequence of the government reforms. There is much that can be done at agency and institutional levels to obviate these effects and to promote a more wholesome educational environment for teachers and pupils alike.

7   Prevention is better than cure
Implications for policy

Introduction

We have argued throughout this book that the sources of stress for teachers lie in the breakdown of traditional trust relations and in the interaction between societal, organisational and personal factors. This is evident in the intensification and deprofessionalisation of teachers' work and in the deterioration of social relationships in workplace cultures. All these impact negatively upon job satisfaction, health and careers (Kelchtermans and Strittmatter, 1999).

Teaching, like many other professions, is inevitably stressful and it is unlikely, even if thought desirable, that it could be made stress free (Sergiovanni, 1999). However, we have seen how the stress that some teachers in this study experience is severely psychologically, physically and emotionally damaging. Such levels of stress are not only personally damaging, but also increasingly costly to the economy. It is clear, then, that policies which effect teachers' work are in need of revision.

Stress, traditionally, has been viewed in personal terms as a 'disease' suffered by individuals. Thus, strategies for its alleviation are aimed at individuals with the intention of changing the worker rather than the work situation (Cox, 1993), what Friedman (1999) describes as indirect 'palliative' strategies for the alleviation of mental and physical symptoms. We have seen many examples of this ideology and approach in our research, with emphasis being placed on caring for and curing the sufferer. However, Handy (1990: 26) argues that:

> Unfortunately, the fact that work problems cannot be resolved easily does not mean that they can be ignored with impunity, as facile solutions may well fail precisely ... because the individually-oriented analyses and intervention strategies proposed by many stress or burnout researchers may simply divert attention from organisational issues and help perpetuate the very problems they are designed to solve.

Since many of the causes of stress lie beyond the control of the individual, we need to look further than approaches to person-focused mediation of stress, past 'timely reaction' and eventual 'rehabilitation' of sufferers (Cox, 1993), to policies which aim to prevent stress occurring through taking account of a range of factors other than personal ones. These are policies and strategies of 'direct action' dealing directly with the basic causes of stress (Friedman, 1999). Current policies and laws on occupational stress emphasise risk reduction and stress prevention (Health and Safety Commission, 1990; Cox, 1993); and research on workplace intervention and stress prevention policy and practice attests to both its efficacy and cost effectiveness when compared with *post hoc* alleviation strategies (Cox, 1993).

Here, we use the lessons learned from our research to inform policies for the prevention of stress in teaching and also identify 'spaces' that teachers can occupy in the defence of their professionalism and health. The study raises implications for policy at three levels: the educational system itself; the school; and the individual.

Level 1: Educational system

The nature of work is changing dramatically in education as it is in other areas of the public and private sector. Growing insecurity, changing forms of authority in the workplace and the new relationship between home and work make changes in social and education policy imperative. After the harsh management styles of the 1990s, which were viewed by some as being appropriate for corporate downsizing, we now have the realisation by some employers that their workforce is the largest of their investments and is also their most valuable asset (Crace, 1999b). New, softer management styles and employer/employee relationships are now emerging in some employment sectors (Benady, 1999). Firms which require flexibility from their workers, are now becoming more flexible themselves by recognising (prompted by the evidence of increasing staff turnover, sickness, low productivity, increasing litigation etc.) that employers must take a large responsibility for their workers' health. Part of that responsibility is appreciating factors in the home/work interface and how these can affect workers' health and productivity. The use of Employee Assistance Programmes and other stress reduction measures in some states in the USA have led the way in achieving new ways of working, litigation prevention and in providing a model for other economies (Cox, 1993). MacLennan (1992), for instance, describes how some USA banking institutions experiencing problems with high turnover, sickness absence and low productivity introduced stress reduction initiatives. These involved employees in the identification of sources of stress and the eliciting of their proposed solutions for change or removal resulting in workers devising initiatives to, 'reduce work–family conflicts including on-site day centres for preschool and school children; maternity leave arrangements; job protection schemes; arrangements for part-time work for returning mothers and fathers;

flexitime and working at home; the provision of "family sick days"; and unpaid leave to be used for spouses or elderly parents' (all cited in Cox, 1993: 72). Murphy and Hurrell (1987) argue that the creation of a worker–management 'stress reduction committee' is a prerequisite for stress prevention policy formation.

To date, policies of educational reform since 1988 have been based largely on distrust of teachers. In our view, such strategies as the recently introduced teacher award ceremonies will achieve little in terms of reinvesting trust in the profession. For improvements in teachers' experience of work and in the quality of education they provide, there needs to be a public restoration of trust in teachers and teaching, a significant part of which is a balanced media image (Kelchtermans and Strittmatter, 1999). As Leiter (1999: 208) explains:

> Constraints on professional prerogatives throughout society and growing criticism of professionals in popular media exacerbate the impact of organizational downsizing and retrenchment on staff members' sense of themselves. The idea of their work as a way in which to make a meaningful contribution is overwhelmed by mundane tasks and perceptions of diminishing service quality.

They also need more autonomy and self-determination as a profession. The newly formed GTC promises to be a professional body which, potentially, has powers for the recruitment, selection and training of teachers. Additionally, it will aim to set professional standards and be responsible for dealing with members who do not meet these standards (Mahony and Hextall, 2000). Such a body could give 'clear expectations to teachers . . . thus heightening professional motivation' (Kelchtermans and Strittmatter, 1999: 307). Hitherto, professional performance and conduct has been subject to scrutiny by Ofsted, headteachers and governors. Reforms in this area of school management have been informed by technical-rational managerialist models and strategies. It is now clear that policies of naming, blaming and shaming and the management styles and systems of Ofsted are increasingly out of step with new management approaches being introduced into the private sector where the 'softer' styles are increasingly becoming established (Benady, 1999). However, there is a softening evident with new initiatives such as light-touch inspections and lengthening the time between inspections (Woods et al., 2000). It is unlikely that Ofsted style inspections which have damaged teachers (see Jeffrey and Woods, 1998 and recent reports of teacher suicides linked to inspections, Mansell, 2000) and have a questionable relationship in raising the quality of education will be replaced with the type of 'no blame' inspections advocated by some (Douglas, 1992) in the USA (Comer et al., 1996) and in the UK (Fitz-Gibbon et al., 1996). Evaluation and accountability systems more in line with stress prevention would resemble a form of school self-evaluation which was becoming widespread in England immediately prior to the introduction of the National Curriculum in 1988. Assessment initiatives, such as records of achievement, combined curriculum development, teacher development, pupil formative and summative assessment and school self-evaluation (see Broadfoot, 1986). Such schemes fostered pupil and teacher ownership of curriculum and assessment and provided wider and more meaningful accountability, particularly at community level.

Currently LEAs are being subjected to the same kind of 'blaming' culture that schools have suffered. They are under threat of being disbanded and replaced with privatised management teams if their performance does not pass Ofsted scrutiny. It is argued that, in many cases, they add little to the quality of teaching and learning in the schools for which they are responsible while consuming costly overheads which are borne by the central state and local taxpayers (Dean, 2000). We have seen in this study the extremely valuable role played by the local authority occupational health manager in stress alleviation for employees. While this role would be retained initially, it would be important for these experienced personnel to become also responsible for the formation and implementation of stress prevention policy, in collaboration with education professionals. However, we feel provision of this or any other type of initiatives in this area would not occur in a privatised system. Additional responsibilities would include the creation of an ombudsperson, whose role operating at local level, would be to mediate disputes and grievances before situations escalated and participants' health deteriorated. At present, the occupational health manager can and does intervene in situations, but often this takes place after much damage has already been done and the intervention is too late. Currently, the relationship between the GTC, teacher unions and LEAs in this respect is unclear. What is apparent is that the provision of individuals with the power and authority to intervene on behalf of teachers is a policy priority.

High trust, high performance relations at work are being achieved in some economies and must serve as a model for our own system. Sennett (1998) argues that the low-trust 'corporate culture is counterproductive, in that it lowers workforce morale, thus ultimately reducing productivity and profits' (Macnicol, 1999: 30). However, Kramer and Tyler (1996) argue that high-performance economies need high-trust institutions in order to cope with high risks. Fukuyama (1995), for instance, argues that in terms of international economic competitiveness the most effective economies have high-trust institutions and societies. Yet the picture of the work cultures of low-trust schooling presented in our analysis is, like Helsby's (1999: 65):

> clearly the antithesis of the vision of the 'new work order' which promises to motivate staff and to unleash their capacity to be innovative and entrepreneurial in responding to customer needs.

In the context of some states in the USA, trust in teachers to implement reform has been retained in 'third wave' educational reform policies. There has been a 'resurgence in and respect for the dignity, quality and sophistication of teachers' practical knowledge and judgement' (Hargreaves and Dawe, 1989: 4–5). Restructuring of schools as recommended by groups such as the USA Carnegie Forum on 'Education and the Economy' would 'respect and support the professionalism of teachers to make decisions in their own classrooms that best met local and state goals while holding teachers accountable for how they did that' (Hargreaves 1994: 241). Murphy and Evertson (1991) suggest components of restructuring which include: school-based management, increased consumer choice, teacher empowerment, and teaching for understanding. The National Governors' Association (1989) recommend that 'curriculum and instruction be redesigned to promote higher order thinking skills and the decentralisation of authority and decision-making to site level, more diverse and differentiated roles for teachers and broader systems of accountability' (cited in Hargreaves, 1994: 241).

It is increasingly clear that the inequitable funding arrangements for primary schools *vis-à-vis* secondary schools (see Campbell, 1989; Thomas, 1990), and the uneven effects of funding of Local Management of Schools, have created winners and losers in the funding process (Bowe et al., 1992). Improved financing would reduce numbers of short-term contracts and redundancies, thus removing uncertainty and insecurity from the experience of many teachers, and also easing divisive atmospheres and cultures of mistrust in schools. Unless the financing of primary education is seriously addressed as a policy priority, no progress can be made in developing initiatives which would reduce teachers' workloads and prevent stress. Increased funding of the system is also important to change the regulations allowing teachers to retire early without suffering financial penalty. New arrangements should be introduced to allow those feeling trapped in a particular phase to retrain for another. Sabbaticals could also be offered to teachers as part of their professional development. MacMahon (2000: 9) notes that the professional development proposals contained in the Green Paper (1998) offer some hope with regard to such initiatives as they:

> seem to promise a new impetus and herald a commitment to providing time to enable teachers to reflect and plan their development. They also advocate encouraging and funding a wide range of education and training opportunities intended to meet individual as well as organisational goals (e.g. professional bursaries, which would make sums of money available direct to teachers, international exchanges and study visits; teacher research scholarships, and development portfolios).

Level 2: School

Friedman (1999) argues that work-related stressors are more important than personal factors or socio-demographic factors in the generation of stress. If negative relationships with leaders, colleagues, pupils and parents are a source of stress in teachers' work, then ways of achieving positive relationships must be incorporated for stress prevention. If some schools are stress producing socially toxic environments, how can we make them 'healthier workplaces'? (ibid.). The first aim of policy making in this area must be to remove the emphasis on the individualisation of stress. Indeed, the HSE state that: the 'work situation itself should be the initial focus of concern' in stress prevention (Parkes and Sparkes, 1998: 1). Handy (1988) argues that the use of individually focused stress alleviation policies and strategies in work settings is 'conceptually naive', and Ganster et al. (1982) 'consider them to be "ethically questionable" as a response to chronic work stress on the grounds that they misattribute responsibility for managing work stress to the individual employee rather than to the organization itself, where it correctly belongs' (Parkes and Sparkes, 1998: 1).

As with Level 1, trust is central to change and trusting relations need to be restored in the workplace cultures of schooling (Fox, 1974). Teachers should be both trusted and valued and these principles should be incorporated in policy. Preventing stress is, for some, directly linked to school improvement strategies (Kelchtermans and Strittmatter, 1999; Miller, 1999). We know from the teacher development literature that school improvement is 'only likely in schools where risk-taking is encouraged within an atmosphere of basic trust and support' (Goodlad, 1984), and where teachers are 'given the basic security of being trusted and valued' (Hargreaves, 1998a: 324). Our case study of a low-stress school showed not only that it successfully prevented high stress levels but was achieving this both in its own and in Ofsted's terms. Damaging stress was prevented by the shared discourse and practice of teamwork and the workplace culture being characterised by *openness, sharing, supporting, understanding* and *realism*. Teamwork breaks down the isolation which causes stress (Kelchtermans and Strittmatter, 1999). Schwarzer and Greenglass (1999: 245–6) argue that:

> When teachers realise after years of stress and unsuccessful coping that they feel burned out, they experience helplessness and resignation, harbour recovery self-doubts, and believe they are incapable of taking instrumental action or mobilizing efficient social support. Burnout, then, becomes itself a determinant of subsequent goal setting and action processes. The vicious cycle continues – unless self-doubts are overcome or social support is provided.

Leithwood et al. (1999: 94) argue that stress and burnout is less likely for teachers who receive *social support* from 'friends, family and colleagues, have opportunities to share professional experiences, and who do not experience feelings of professional isolation. Burnout is also less likely for teachers who receive recognition for their efforts and achievements'. *Organizational support* is important too in reducing stress and burnout and includes 'opportunities to change assignments or types of work, and to work within flexible, non-hierarchical, administrative structures. Access to adequate physical facilities that can be used in flexible ways and access to support personnel (also a form of support) reduce the likelihood of burnout as does having an influence on decisions and job security' (ibid.).

Shared missions, core values, aims and goals (Kelchtermans and Strittmatter, 1999) are the basis of collaborative cultures of care and they do not come about by accident. Policies at school level are needed to create cultures of this type. The work of Nias et al. (1989), Acker, (1999) and Woods (1995b) detail the social processes at work in the formation and maintenance of these cultures and this should form the basis of policy. Of course, the increased funding of primary education recommended above would be instrumental in facilitating the development of collaborative relationships. For instance we are aware of some of the educational disadvantages of non-contact time (see Hargreaves, 1994), but it also has many advantages and should, we argue, be a right for all primary teachers. Teachers released from the classroom would be enabled to develop collaborative relationships with their colleagues in informal and formal settings. If successful restructuring depends upon shared decision-making and teamwork, then time should be devoted to teachers acquiring these skills during the school day rather than leaving this learning to chance.

A culture of learning by problem-solving would be one in which it was acceptable to admit mistakes and see them as opportunities to learn and not as an indication of professional incompetence. Putting mistakes right would become a collective rather than individual process. This form of culture would be one most likely to foster critical self-reflection which some have advocated channelling into action research as a way of maintaining meaning in teaching, professional development and stress prevention (Vulliamy and Webb, 1991). Both Huberman (1993) and Cherniss (1995) recognised the importance of teachers becoming involved in innovations in order to alleviate stress in their work. The paradox noted here by Little (2000) is that in current restructuring it is teacher involvement in state sponsored (and often legislated) reform innovations which is the source of the stress. It would be important, therefore, to seek ways for teachers to become involved in 'meaningful' innovations in which they can experience ownership of the intiative. This is particularly urgent with a rapidly ageing workforce. Much more attention needs paying to job satisfaction and these forms of professional development (Friedman, 1999).

We have seen how important informal social support is in the alleviation of stress. Stress prevention measures may involve formal supports such as 'critical friends', 'mentor', 'pairing schemes' and 'buddy' systems being set in place. These supports are important for all teachers but particularly for new and younger teachers who may experience a greater sense of exhaustion than their more experienced colleagues (Friedman, 1999). Neither must these initiatives be restricted to teachers. Headteachers, too, would benefit from emotional and practical support from appropriately experienced peers throughout their careers, but particularly in the early stages of first headship. While current official initiatives recognise the importance of mentoring in induction, the purpose of the mentor/mentee relationship is seen strictly in instrumental terms of the development of professional competencies such as classroom management, assessment and curriculum planning (Tickle, 1999). This ignores the important social and emotional support which can be provided in such systems. Given the high attrition rate in beginning teachers, these aspects should, perhaps, be prioritised in education policy aimed at stress prevention and teacher retention.

We have shown how poor relationships between teachers and pupils can be a source of stress and low self-esteem. Also, how caring emotional bonds with pupils can increase teachers' self-esteem, confidence and sense of efficacy, thereby reducing stress. Here smaller class sizes would give teachers opportunities to divide their attention and help them develop appropriate and educative warm relationships with pupils (Hargreaves, 1998a). In this respect, while the integration of EBD children in mainstream classes was supported by our teachers, it was, in some cases, at the expense of the teacher being able to give attention to all members of the class and covering the National Curriculum. Financial support is needed for this integration and for those children who are statemented in order to preserve the mental health of the teacher. Financial provision would also enable increased ancillary support in classrooms and with the bureaucratic workload. It is important here that extra LSAs are employed to support teachers rather than replace them (Marr, 2000). The government seemed committed to reducing teacher workload (Coopers and Lybrand, 1998), but this commitment now needs translating into policy and provision.

Many of the stressful incidents that were reported in our research were owing to poor relationships between teachers and parents. Indeed, the emotional geography (Hargreaves, 1999a) of teacher/parent relationships seems set against harmonious and collaborative enterprise. However, the development of educative relationships with parents and the community and their active involvement in the teaching and learning process (Bastiani, 1987) would foster more productive relationships and reduce stress. There are some outstanding examples of what can be achieved in this respect (O'Grady, 1995).

This study has shown the centrality of the headteacher in inducing or preventing stress in teachers. Indeed, the headteacher is the representative of an employer who has a statutory duty of care which is embodied in HSE laws. The employer's duty to employees is to support and train them and to allocate work appropriately. The headteacher is at the centre of low-stress collaborative workplace cultures and has the most important influence on school ethos and 'institutional bias' (Pollard, 1985). Headteachers, therefore, need to be knowledgeable about the sources of stress in teaching and how to prevent them. This is most likely to be achieved if there is a significant shift in values in the selection and training of headteachers. At present, as with inspections, the appointment and professional development of headteachers, evident in such schemes as HEADLAMP (Blandford and Squire, 2000) and the NPQH, are driven by technical-rational managerialist organisational ideology. As MacMahon (2000: 9) points out, 'the National Standards for Headteachers (Teacher Training Agency, 1997) state that heads should be able to "work under pressure and to deadlines" not that they should seek to manage or control the pressures in the workplace'. There is no provision in such training for developing the emotional understanding vital for leadership and stress prevention (Hargreaves, 1998a). Headteacher training, therefore, must not only include a main focus on leadership and the emotions, but must also deal with the practical and legal aspects of personnel management. An understanding of teachers not just in the workplace but also knowing how the emotional interactions of the home/work interface impact on professional work is needed. There is often a 'delicate balance between assisting individuals and protecting and promoting the interests of the organization' (Cox, 1993: 67). Headteachers need training in order to develop the skills and understanding to maintain that balance.

Headteachers need to know when and how to give 'back-up' (Beatty, 1999) to their teachers. They need to understand, too, their teachers' capacity for work to enable them, as transformational leaders (Sleegers, 1999: 255), to 'create educationally inviting settings that also drive teachers to a higher level of concern, increased motivation, and reduced stress. In other words, expanding the innovative capacity of a school can provide a buffer against teacher burnout'.

Stress is experienced when teachers feel they are losing or are not in control of their personal and professional lives. Employers and managers must understand that stress prevention involves handing some control back to teachers. Lortie (1975), for example, warns of the stressful implications of removing teachers from policy making and the control of work. Many argue the importance of including teachers in decision-making to prevent stress by increasing their sense of efficacy, self-esteem, control and professional confidence (see for example, Rudow, 1999). However, involvement can overload and has 'the potential to enervate rather than energise the teaching staff' (ibid.: 152). Headteachers, therefore, need to know when, and on what issues, this involvement should take place. As we have shown, teachers forced into 'contrived collegiality' (Hargreaves, 1994), for example by being asked to discuss trivial issues at meetings which divert them from their main educational role, is a recipe for frustration and stress.

The involvement of the whole staff in an annual stress audit could help to develop these kinds on understandings.

Level 3: Individual

Our research suggests that one of the main impacts of teacher stress is a profound change in the 'self' involving reduced personal and professional confidence and lowered self-esteem. As a consequence, teachers experience a sense of greatly reduced efficacy and their commitment to the workplace is weakened. This impacts negatively on the quality of teaching. In the most extreme cases the teachers are absent from school for long periods. This process can be seen graphically in the narratives of stressed (and 'bullied') teachers, those undergoing competency procedures, and in the case study of teachers working in (and leaving) a 'failing school'. These teachers' workplace conditions negatively affected workplace commitment; though not necessarily commitment to teaching. These teachers often remained in post giving a reduced performance or having prolonged periods absent from work, then either returning with a greatly reduced commitment or leaving teaching. This was particularly pronounced in the 'failing school'.

Teachers often regarded their failure to cope with stress as their own fault (Friedman, 1999). Such feelings can be countered by the provision of knowledge about sources of stress, the identification of somatic, psychological and emotional symptoms and coping strategies. There are no readymade recipes for success here, but this approach may help to support other preventative measures. Seeking this kind of knowledge when already ill is leaving things rather too late.

The diminished personal accomplishment experienced as a result of stress often leads to the individual developing a lower commitment to the organisation (Rosenholtz, 1989; Leiter, 1999). However, in restructuring initiatives more and more is asked of teachers in the drive for targets and raised 'standards'. In restructuring, teachers must reinvent not only their schools but also themselves. Miller (1999) argues that restructuring may not necessarily be at odds with teachers' own needs for career enrichment, while Smylie (1999) argues that there are three interconnected psychological needs associated with teachers' work – meaningfulness, self-determination and the accomplishment of valued goals. Rudow (1999) sees professional development as a buffer against stress. There is a need, then, for career-long professional learning and development both inside and outside the organisation. As argued earlier, basic feelings of trust and security are important for achieving professional learning (Kelchtermans and Strittmatter, 1999). Professional development, like successful teaching, also requires the teacher to have positive self-esteem and a greater locus of internal control (Riseborough, 1981).

In order to teach effectively, teachers must not only feel psychologically and emotionally 'comfortable', they must also have some sense of self-efficacy. They must feel their professional work is bringing about positive change in their pupils. They need to know that, for instance, they are making a difference in the lives of children they are teaching and that they are learning. Teachers also need to 'feel wanted, important and in some ways unique, they need to have these needs affirmed by those with whom they live and work' (Rudow, 1999). In order to have these emotional needs fulfilled, they need feedback on their professional practice. This can be achieved through such arrangements as 'peer coaching' or team teaching, rather than forms of monitoring attached to managerial concerns and inspection agendas. The latter initiatives, as we have shown in the study, are often inappropriate for professional learning and development of individuals. Miller (1999: 143) argues that time needs setting aside for 'planning together, teaching together, and talking together. Peer observation and consultation contribute to a shared professional culture in which risks are encouraged, mistakes acknowledged, and learning scrutinized.' Teachers need regular feedback, recognition and praise from headteachers, too, in order to increase feelings of self-efficacy, professional confidence and organisational commitment. Leaders are needed who can help teachers to succeed and reward that success. Areas of weakness identified in this process should form the basis for further professional development rather than the focus for blame and censure. The openness of a collaborative culture would also make it possible for individuals to reveal mistakes and feelings of inadequacy and stress without these being taken as symptoms of incompetence. Addressing these issues would be both a collective and individual task. The *Green Paper*'s (DfEE, 1998b) proposals for the award of performance related pay look unlikely to fulfil the feedback role we have described. While appraisal of this type is likely to reward the efforts of some, it promises to be divisive, marginalising the efforts and accomplishments of the many, thus not supporting *every* individual's sense of self-efficacy, professional confidence, organizational commitment or professional development, thereby undermining collegiality. Teachers and headteachers alike fear that, in the proposed arrangements for threshold assessment of teachers, support will become surveillance, and teamwork and professional development will be replaced by suspicion and 'snooping' (Barnard and Henry, 2000).

Clearly, there is much that can be done at all three levels of government, institution and individual to obviate the rising tide of teacher stress and yield more educational reward from teaching for all concerned. If much of it arises in the first instance from the particular restructuring programme adopted by government, we have shown that it is not an inevitable consequence – there are things that schools and teachers can do to alleviate the effect. However, the biggest shift that could be made would be one that involved moving from a competitive, marketing, managerialist discourse to a more co-operative, humanist, democratic one.

References

Acker, S. (1992) 'Creating careers: Women teachers at work', *Curriculum Inquiry*, 22(2): 141–63.

Acker, S. (1999) *The Realities of Teachers' Work: Never a Dull Moment*, London: Cassell.

Alexander, J. (1989) *The Modern Reconstruction of Classical Thought*, London: Routledge & Kegan Paul.

Ameghino, J. (1998) 'Add stress to your CV', in *The Guardian*, 15 September: 17.

Apple, M. (1986) *Teachers and Texts*, London: Routledge & Kegan Paul.

Argyris, C. (1970) *Intervention Theory and Method: A Behaviour Science View*, Reading, MA: Addison-Wesley.

Association of Teachers and Lecturers (1996) *Bullying at Work: a Guide for Teachers*, London: ATL.

Ball, S. J. (1987) *The Micro-Politics of the School: Towards a Theory of School Organisation*, London: Methuen.

Ball, S. J. (1988) 'Staff relations during the teachers' industrial action: context, conflict and proletarianisation', *British Journal of Sociology of Education*, 9(3): 289–306.

Ball, S. J. (1994) *Education Reform: A Critical and Post-structural Approach*, Buckingham: Open University Press.

Ball, S. J. (1998) 'Educational studies, policy entrepreneurship and social theory, in Slee, R. and Weiner, G. with Tomlinson, S. (eds) *School Effectiveness for Whom? Challenges to the School Effectiveness and School Improvement Movements*, London: Falmer Press.

Ball, S. J. and Bowe, R. (1992) 'Subject departments and the implementation of the National Curriculum policy: An overview of the issues', *Journal of Curriculum Studies*, 24(2): 97–115.

Ball, S. J. and Goodson, I. F. (eds) (1985) *Teachers' Lives and Careers*, Lewes: Falmer.

Barnard, N. (1999) 'New TTA chief calls for "radical" change', *The Times Educational Supplement*, 17 March: 1.

Barnard, N. and Henry, J. (2000) 'Total support for fight against "snoops"' charter', *The Times Educational Supplement*, 28 April: 5.

Bartlett, D. (1998) *Stress: Perspectives and Processes*, Buckingham: Open University Press.

Bastiani, J. (1987) *Parents and Schools*, Volumes 1 & 2, Windsor: NFER Nelson.

Beatty, B. (1999) 'Teachers and their leaders: The emotionality of teachers' relationships with administrators', presented to the *International Study Association on Teachers and Teaching*, Dublin, Ireland, June.

Beck, U. (1992) *Risk Society*, London: Sage.

Becker, H. (1966) 'Introduction' to Shaw, C. R., *The Jack-Roller*, Chicago: University of Chicago Press.

Becker, H. (1977) 'Personal change in adult life', in Cosin, B. R. et al. (eds) *School and Society* (2nd edition), London: Routledge & Kegan Paul.

Benady, A. (1999) 'Why firms are bringing humanity into work', *The Guardian, Jobs*, 31 July: 18–19.

Berger, P. L. (1964) 'The human shape of work', in Esland, G., Salaman, G. and Speakman, G. (eds) (1975) *People and Work*, Edinburgh: Holmes McDougal/The Open University Press.

Beynon, J. (1984) 'Sussing-out teachers – pupils as data gatherers', in Hammersley, M. and Woods, P. (eds) *Life in School*, Milton Keynes: Open University Press.

Biott, C. and Nias, J. (eds) (1992) *Working and Learning Together for Change*, Buckingham: Open University Press.

Blandford, S. and Squire, L. (2000) 'An evaluation of the teacher training agency headteacher leadership and management programme (HEADLAMP)', *Educational Management and Administration*, 28(1): 21–32.

Blase, J. (1991) *The Politics of Life in Schools: Power, Conflict and Cooperation*, London: Sage.

Blase, J. and Anderson, G. (1995) *The Micropolitics of Educational Leadership*, London: Cassell.

Bloome, D. and Willett, J. (1991) 'Towards a micropolitics of classroom interaction', in Blase, J. (ed) *The Politics of Life in Schools*, London: Sage.

Bowe, R., Ball, S. J. with Gold, A. (1992) *Reforming Education and Changing Schools: Case Studies in Policy Sociology*, London: Routledge.

Brand, K.-W. (1990) 'Cyclical aspects of new social movements: Waves of cultural criticism and mobilization cycles of new middle class radicalism', in Dalton, J. D. and Kuechler, M. (eds) *Challenging the Political Order: New Social and Political Movements in Western Democracies*, Cambridge: Polity Press.

Broadfoot, P. (ed.) (1986) *Profiles and Records of Achievement: A Review of Issues and Practice*, Eastbourne: Holt Rinehart & Winston.

Broadfoot, P. and Osborn, M. (1988) 'What professional responsibility means to teachers: national contexts and classroom constants', in *British Journal of Sociology of Education*, 9(3): 265–88.

Brown, M. and Ralph, S. (1998) 'Change-linked stress in British teachers', paper presented to the *British Educational Research Association* Conference, Queen's University Belfast.

Brown, P. (1990) 'The third wave: education and the ideology of parentocracy', *British Journal of Sociology of Education*, 11(1): 65–87.

Cabinet Office (1998) *Managing Attendance in the Public Sector*: London: Cabinet Office.

Cains, R. A. and Brown, C. R. (1998) 'Newly qualified teachers: a comparative analysis of the perceptions held by B.Ed. and PGCE-trained primary teachers of the level and frequency of stress experienced during the first year of teaching', *Educational Psychology*, 18(1): 257–70.

Caldwell, B. and Spinks, J. (1988) *The Self-Managing School*, London: Falmer Press.

Campbell, R. J. (1989) 'Teacher time, activity-led staffing and formula funding: A prospect for improving primary schools', *Education 3–13*, 7(2): 3–8.

Campbell, R. J. and St J. Neill, S. R. (1994) *Primary Teachers at Work*, London: Routledge.

Carlyle, D. (1998) 'Walking on eggshells: the impact of stress on teachers' family lives', paper presented at the *British Educational Research Association* Conference, Queen's University, Belfast, September.

Carlyle, D. (1999) 'Between the devil and the deep blue sea: The emotion of self-renewal after stress-related illness', paper presented at the *British Educational Research Association* Conference, University of Sussex, September.

Castells, M. (1997) *The Power of Identity*, Oxford: Basil Blackwell.

Castells, M. (1998) *The End of Millennium*, Oxford: Basil Blackwell.

Central Advisory Council for Education (CACE) (1967) *Children and their Primary Schools* (The Plowden Report), London: HMSO.

Cherniss, C. (1995) *Beyond Burnout: Helping Teachers, Nurses, Therapists and Lawyers Recover from Stress and Disillusionment*, New York: Routledge.

Cockburn, A. D. (1996) *Teaching Under Pressure: Looking at Primary Teacher Stress*, London: Falmer Press.

Comer, J. P., Haynes, N. M., Joyner, E. T. and Ben-Avi, M. (1996) *Rallying the Whole Village: The Comer Process for Reforming Education*, New York: Teachers' College Press.

Convery, A. (1999) 'Listening to teachers' stories: are we sitting comfortably?', *International Qualitative Studies in Education*, 12(2): 131–46.

Cooper, C. and Hoel, H. (2000) *Destructive Interpersonal Conflict and Bullying at Work: Key Findings*, February, School of Management, University of Manchester Institute of Science and Technology.

Coopers and Lybrand (1998) *Reducing the Bureaucratic Burden on Teachers* (*Research Report No. 41*), London: DfEE.

Cox, T. (1993) *Stress Research and Stress Management: Putting Theory to Work*, Norwich: Health and Safety Executive.

Crace, J. (1999a) 'Stressed out at the age of seven', *The Guardian, Education*, Tuesday 20 July: 2.

Crace, J. (1999b) 'Is it care and share or hire and fire?', *The Guardian, Jobs*, 16 October: 34–5.

Dadds, M. (1993) 'The feeling of thinking in professional self-study', *Educational Action Research*, 1(2): 287–303.

Dale, R. (1989) *The State and Education Policy*, Milton Keynes: Open University Press.

Dalton, J. D. and Kuechler, M. (eds) (1990) *Challenging the Political Order: New Social and Political Movements in Western Democracies*, Cambridge: Polity Press.

Dainton, S. (1999) 'Think again, Mr Blunkett', *Forum*, 41(2): 43–5.

David, M. (1992) 'Parents and the state: how has social research informed education reforms?' in Arnot, M. and Barton, L. (eds) *Voicing Concerns: sociological perspectives on contemporary education reforms*, Wallingford: Triangle.

Dean, C. (2000) 'Firm is hired to run ailing services', *The Times Educational Supplement*, 24 March: 10.

Dearing, R. (1994) *The National Curriculum and Its Assessment, Final Report*, London, SCAA.

De Heus, P. and Diekstra, F. W. (1999) 'Do teachers burn out more easily? A comparison of teachers with other social professions on work stress and burnout symptoms', in Vandenberghe, R. and Huberman, A. M. *Understanding and Preventing Teacher Burnout*, Cambridge: Cambridge University Press.

Densmore, K. (1987) 'Professionalism, proletarianization and teachers' work', in Popkewitz, T. (ed.) *Critical Studies in Teacher Education*, Lewes: Falmer Press.

Denzin, N. (1984) *On Understanding Emotion*, San Francisco: Jossey-Bass.

Department for Education and Employment (1998a) *Statistics of Education, Teachers, England and Wales, 1998 Edition*, London: The Stationery Office.

Department for Education and Employment (1998b) *Teachers Meeting the Challenge of Change*, London: DfEE.

Department for Education and Employment (1999) 'DfEE Research', *Education Journal*, May, p. 31.

Department for Education and Employment and Ofsted (1995) *The Improvement of Failing Schools: UK Policy and Practice 1993–1995*, London: DfEE and Ofsted.

Department of Education and Science (1992) *Curriculum Organisation and Classroom Practice in Primary Schools: A Discussion Paper*, London: DES Information Branch.

Diamond, M. (1993) *The Unconscious Life of Organizations: Interpreting Organizational Identity*, West Port, CT: Quorum Books.

Dinham, S. K. (1992) 'Human perspectives on the resignation of teachers from the New South Wales public school system: Towards a model of teacher persistence', unpublished PhD thesis, University of New England: Armidale.

Dinham, S. K. and Scott, C. (1996) *The Teacher 2000 Project: A Study of Teacher Satisfaction, Motivation and Health*, Nepean: University of Western Sydney.

Docking, J. W. (1987) *Control and Discipline in Schools: Perspectives and Approaches* (2nd edn), London: Harper & Row.

Douglas, M. (1992) *Risk and Blame: Essays in Cultural Theory*, London: Routledge.

Draper, J. (1993) 'We're back with Gobbo: the re-establishment of gender relations following a school merger', in Woods, P. and Hammersley, M. (eds) *Gender and Ethnicity in Schools; Ethnographic Accounts*, London: Routledge.

Dubberley, W. S. (1993) 'Humour as resistance', in Woods, P. and Hammersley, M. (eds) *Gender and Ethnicity in Schools: Ethnographic Accounts*, London: Routledge.

Dunham, S. (1984) *Stress in Teaching*, Beckenham: Croom Helm.

Durkheim, E. (1956) *Education and Sociology*, trans. Fox, S. D., Glencoe, New York: Free Press.

Elias, N. (1987) *Involvement and Detachment*, Oxford: Basil Blackwell.

Elster, J. (1989) *The Cement of Society*, Cambridge: Cambridge University Press.

Evans, L. (1992) 'Teachers' morale and satisfaction: The importance of school-specific factors', paper presented at the *British Educational Research Association* Conference, University of Liverpool, September.

Evans, L., Packwood, A., St J. Neill, S. R. and Campbell, R. J. (1994) *The Meaning of Infant Teachers' Work*, London: Routledge.

Evetts, J. (1987) 'Becoming career ambitious: the career strategies of married women who became primary headteachers in the 1960s and 1970s', *Educational Review*, 39(1): 15–29.

Field, T. (1996) *Bully in Sight: How to Predict, Resist, Challenge and Combat Workplace Bullying*, Harwell: Success Unlimited.

Field, T. (2000) *The National Workplace Bullying Advice Line*, http://www.successun-limited.co.uk

Fineman, S. (1995) 'Stress, emotion and intervention', in Newton, T. with Handy, J. and Fineman, S. *'Managing' Stress: Emotion and Power at Work*, London: Sage.

Fink, D. (1999) '"Deadwood Didn't Kill Itself": A Pathology of Failing Schools', *Educational Management and Administration*, 27(2): 131–41.

Fisher, P. (1995) 'Conditions are the key to discontent', *The Times Educational Supplement*, 27 January: 12.

Fisher, P. (1996) 'Long odds on survival', *The Times Educational Supplement*, 2 February: 10.

Fitz, J., Halpin, D. and Power, S. (1994) 'Implementation research and education policy: practice and prospects', *British Journal of Educational Studies*, 42(1): 53–69.

Fitz-Gibbon, C. T. (1996) *Monitoring Education: Indicators, Quality and Effectiveness*, London: Cassell.

Ford, M. E. (1992) *Motivating Humans, Goals, Emotions and Personal Agency Beliefs*, London: Sage.

Foucault, M. (1977) *Discipline and Punish: The Birth of the Prison*, New York: Pantheon Books.

Fox, A. (1974) *Beyond Contract: Work, Power and Trust Relations*, London: Faber & Faber.

Friedman, A. L. (1977) *Industry and Labour: Class Struggle at Work and Monopoly Capitalism*, London: Macmillan.

Friedman, I. A. (1991) 'High- and low-burnout schools: School culture aspects of teacher burnout', *Journal of Educational Research*, 84: 325–33.

Friedman, I. A. (1999) 'Turning our schools into a healthier workplace: Bridging between professional self-efficacy and professional demands', in Vandenberghe, R. and Huberman, A. M. (eds) *Understanding and Preventing Teacher Burnout* Cambridge: Cambridge University Press.

Fukuyama, F. (1995) *Trust: The Social Virtues and the Creation of Prosperity*, London: Hamish Hamilton.

Fullan, M. (1991) *The New Meaning of Educational Change*, New York: Teachers College Press.

Furedi, F. (1999) 'When trust slips', *The Times Higher Education Supplement*, November 12: 37.

Gambetta, D. (1988) 'Can we trust trust?' in Gambetta, D. (ed.) *Trust: Making and Breaking Cooperative Relationships*, Oxford: Basil Blackwell.

Ganster, D., Mayes, B., Sime, W. and Tharp, G. (1982) 'Managing organizational stress: A field experiment', *Journal of Applied Psychology*, 67: 533–42.

Gardner, J. A. and Oswald, A. J. (1999) 'The determinants of job-satisfaction in Britain', a summary of the research at http://www.warwick.ac.uk/news/pr/business/82

Garril, S. (compiler) (1998) Help!: Directory of National Self-Help Groups and Support Organizations, Blackpool: G-Text (g-text@blackpool.net).

Gewirtz, S. (1996) 'Post-welfarism and the reconstruction of teachers' work', paper presented at the *British Educational Research Association* Conference, University of Lancaster, September.

Giddens, A. (1990) *The Consequences of Modernity*, Cambridge: Polity.

Giddens, A. (1991) *Modernity and Self-Identity*, Cambridge: Polity.

Glaser, B. G. and Strauss, A. L. (1967) *The Discovery of Grounded Theory*, Chicago: Aldine.

Goffman, E. (1952) 'On cooling the mark out: Some aspects of adaptation to failure', *Psychiatry*, 15(4): 451–63.

Goffman, E. (1959) *The Presentation of Self in Everyday Life*, New York: Doubleday.

Goffman, E. (1963) *Stigma: Notes on the Management of Spoiled Identity*, Englewood Cliffs, NJ: Prentice-Hall.

Goffman, E. (1968) *Asylums*, Harmondsworth: Penguin.

Goodlad, J. (1984) *A Place Called School*, New York: McGraw-Hill.

Gouldner, A. W. (1955) *Patterns of Industrial Bureaucracy*, London, Routledge & Kegan Paul.

Gouldner, A. W. (1965) *Wildcat Strike*, New York: Harper & Row.

Grace, G. (1991) 'The state and the teachers: Problems in teacher supply, retention and morale', in Grace, G. and Lawn, M. (eds) *Teacher Supply and Teacher Quality: Issues for the 1990s*, Multilingual Matters: Clevedon, Avon.

Grace, G. (1995) *School Leadership: Beyond Education Management, An Essay in Policy Scholarship*, London: Falmer Press.

Hammersley, M. and Atkinson, P. (1995) *Ethnography: Principles in Practice*, (2nd edn), London: Routledge.

Handy, J. (1988) 'Theoretical and methodological problems within occupational stress and burnout research', *Human Relations*, 41: 351–69.

Handy, J. (1990) *Occupational Stress in a Caring Profession*, Aldershot: Avebury.

Handy, J. (1995) 'Rethinking stress: Seeing the collective', in Newton, T., with Handy, J. and Fineman, S. *'Managing' Stress: Emotion and Power at Work*, London: Sage.

Hargreaves, A. (1978) 'The significance of classroom coping strategies', in Barton, L. and Meighan, R. (eds) *Sociological Interpretations of Schooling and Classrooms*, Driffield: Nafferton.

Hargreaves, A. (1993) 'Time and teachers' work: an analysis of the intensification thesis', in Gomm, R. and Woods, P. (eds) *Educational Research in Action*, London: Paul Chapman.

Hargreaves, A. (1994) *Changing Teachers, Changing Times: Teachers' Work and Culture in the Postmodern World*, London: Cassell.

Hargreaves, A. (1998a) 'The emotional politics of teaching and teacher development: with implications for educational leadership', *International Journal of Leadership in Education*, 1(4): 315–36.

Hargreaves, A. (1998b) 'Review symposium', *British Journal of Sociology of Education*, 19(3): 419–23.

Hargreaves, A. (1998c) 'The emotional practice of teaching', *Teaching and Teacher Education*, 14(8): 835–54.

Hargreaves, A. (1999a) 'Teaching in a box: Emotional geographies of teaching', Keynote Address presented to the *International Study Association on Teachers and Teaching*, Dublin, Ireland, June.

Hargreaves, A. (1999b) 'The psychic rewards (and annoyances) of teaching', in Hammersley, M. (ed.) *Researching School Experience: Ethnographic Studies of Teaching and Learning*, London and New York: Routledge.

Hargreaves, A. and Dawe, R. (1989) 'Paths of professional development: contrived collegiality, collaborative culture and the case of peer coaching', unpublished manuscript, Toronto: Ontario Institute for Studies in Education.

Hargreaves, D. H. (1994) 'The new professionalism: the synthesis of professional and institutional development', *Teaching and Teacher Education*, 10(4): 423–38.

Hargreaves, D. H. and Hopkins, D. (1991) *The Empowered School: the Management and Practice of Development Planning*, London, Cassell.

Healy, G. (1999) 'Structuring commitments in interrupted careers: Career breaks, commitment and the life cycle in teaching', *Gender Work and Organization*, 6(4): 185–201.

Health and Safety Commission (1990) *Managing Occupational Stress: a Guide for Managers and Teachers in the Schools Sector*, London: HMSO.

Helsby, G. (1999) *Changing Teachers' Work: The Reform of Secondary Schooling*, Buckingham: The Open University Press.

Hochschild, A. R. (1993) *The Managed Heart: The Commercialization of Human Feeling*, Berkeley: University of California Press.

Howson, J. (1998) 'Situations Vacant', School Management Section, *The Times Educational Supplement*, 23 January: 24.

Howson, J. (1999) 'Male primary teachers still elusive', *Briefing Research Focus*, *The Times Educational Supplement*, 2 April: 19.

Huberman, A. M. (1993) *The Lives of Teachers*, London: Cassell.

Inglis, F. (1989) 'Managerialism and morality' in Carr, W. (ed.) *Quality in Teaching: Arguments for a Reflective Profession*, Lewes: Falmer Press.

International Labour Office (1991) *Teachers: Challenges of the 1990s: Second Joint Meeting on Conditions of Work of Teachers*, Geneva: ILO.

Jeffrey, B. (1998) 'The intensification of primary teachers' work through new forms of accountability', paper presented to the *European Educational Research Association* Conference, University of Ljubljana, Slovenia, September.

Jeffrey, B. and Woods, P. (1995) 'The role of humour in creating a discourse', paper presented to the *International Society for Humour Studies* Conference, Birmingham, July.

Jeffrey, B and Woods, P. (1996) 'Feeling deprofessionalized: the social construction of emotions during an Ofsted inspection', *Cambridge Journal of Education*, 26(3): 325–43.

Jeffrey, B. and Woods, P. (1998) *Testing Teachers: The Effect of School Inspections on Primary Teachers*, London: Falmer Press.

Johnston, J., Mckeowan, E. and McEwen, A. (1999) 'Choosing Primary Teaching as a Career: the perspectives of males and females in training', *Journal of Education for Teaching*, 25(1): 55–64.

Kelchtermans, G. (1995a) 'Teacher stress and burnout': Summary of the conference of *J. Jacobs Foundation* at Marbach Castle, 2–4 November 1995.

Kelchtermans, G. (1995b) 'Teacher stress and burnout': reflections from a biographical perspective on teacher development', paper presented at Conference on *Teacher Burnout*, Marbach, November.

Kelchtermans, G. (1996) 'Teacher vulnerability: understanding its moral and political roots', *Cambridge Journal of Education*, 26(3): 307–23.

Kelchtermans, G. and Strittmatter, A. (1999) 'Beyond individual burnout: A perspective for improved schools. Guidelines for the prevention of burnout', in Vandenberghe, R. and Huberman, A. M. (eds) *Understanding and Preventing Teacher Burnout*, Cambridge: Cambridge University Press.

Kramer, R. M. and Tyler, T. R. (1996) *Trust in Organizations: Frontiers of Theory and Research*, London: Sage.

Kreisberg, S. (1992) *Transforming Power: Domination, Empowerment and Education*, Albany: State University of New York Press.

Kriesi, H., Koopmans, R., Dyvendak, J. W. and Guigni, M. G. (1995) *New Social Movements in Western Europe*, Minneapolis, MN: University of Minnesota Press.

Kyriacou, C. (1980a) 'Stress, health and schoolteachers: A comparison with other professions', *Cambridge Journal of Education*, 10(2): 154–8.

Kyriacou, C. (1980b) 'Sources of stress among British teachers: The contribution of job factors and personality factors', in Cooper, C. L. and Marshall, J. (eds) *White Collar and Professional Stress*, London: John Wiley.

Kyriacou, C. and Sutcliffe, J. (1979) 'Teacher stress and satisfaction', *Educational Research*, 21(2): 89–96.

Lawn, M. (1995) 'Restructuring teaching in the USA and England: moving towards the differentiated, flexible teacher', *Journal of Education Policy*, 10(4): 347–60.

Lawrence, J. and Steed, D. (1986) Primary school perception of disruptive behaviour, *Educational Studies*, 12(2): 147–57.

Lazarus, R. S. (1990) 'Stress, coping and illness', in Friedman, H. S. (ed.) *Personality and Disease*, New York: John Wiley.

Leiter, M. P. (1999) 'Burnout among teachers as a crisis in psychological contracts', in Vandenberghe, R. and Huberman, A. M. (eds) *Understanding and Preventing Teacher Burnout*, Cambridge: Cambridge University Press.

Leithwood, K. A., Menzies, T., Jantzi, D. and Leithwood, J. (1999) 'Teacher burnout: A critical challenge for leaders of restructuring schools', in Vandenberghe, R. and Huberman, A. M. *Understanding and Preventing Teacher Burnout*, Cambridge: Cambridge University Press.

Lewis, H. B. (1971) *Shame and Guilt in Neurosis*, New York: International Universities Press.

Little, J. W. (1990) 'The persistence of privacy: autonomy and initiative in teachers' professional relations', *Teachers' College Record*, 91(4): 509–36.

Little, J. W. (2000) 'Emotionality and career commitment in the context of rational reforms', paper presented at the *American Educational Research Association* Conference, New Orleans, April.

Lortie, D. (1975) *The School Teacher: A Sociological Study*, Chicago: University of Chicago Press.

Maclean, R. (1992) *Teachers' Career and Promotional Patterns*, London: Falmer.

Maclean, R. and McKenzie, P. (eds) (1991) *Australian Teachers' Careers*, Hawthorn, Victoria: ACER.

MacLennan, B. W. (1992) 'Stressor reduction: An organizational alternative to individual stress management', in Quick, J. C., Murphy, L. R. and Hurrell, J. J. (eds) *Stress and Well-Being at Work: Assessments and Interventions for Occupational Mental Health*, Washington, DC: American Psychological Association.

MacLeod, D. (1998) 'Happy days are here again?', *The Guardian, Education*, 29 September: 4.

MacLeod, D. (1999) 'Strugglers thrown a lifeline', *The Guardian, Education*, 22 June: 2.

MacLeod, D. and Meikle, J. (1994) Education changes 'making heads quit', *The Guardian*, 1 September: 6.

MacMahon, A. (2000) 'Managing teacher stress to enhance pupil learning', paper presented at the *American Educational Research Association* Conference, New Orleans, April.

Macnicol, J. (1999) 'A review of Sennett, R. The corrosion of character: The personal consequences of work in the new capitalism', *The Times Higher Education Supplement*, 30 April: 30.

Mahony, P. and Hextall, I. (2000) *Reconstructing Teaching: Standards, Performance and Accountability*, London: Routledge.

Mansell, W. (2000) 'Inquests link four deaths to inspection', *The Times Educational Supplement*, 21 April: 1.

Marr, A. (2000) 'A very visible means of support', *The Times Educational Supplement*, 28 April: 22.

Menter, I., Muschamp, Y., Nicholls, P., Ozga, J. with Pollard, A. (1997) *Work and Identity in the Primary School*, Buckingham: Open University Press.

Menter, I. and Thomson, D. with Ross, A., Hutchings, M. and Bedford, D. (1999) 'Leaving and joining London's teaching force', paper presented at the *British Educational Research Association* Conference, University of Sussex, Brighton, September.

Miller, L. (1999) 'Reframing teacher burnout in the context of school reform and teacher development in the United States', in Vandenberghe, R. and Huberman, A. M. (eds) *Understanding and Preventing Teacher Burnout*, Cambridge: Cambridge University Press.

Milne, S. (1998) 'Two million suffer job-linked illness', *The Guardian*, 21 March: 11.

Misztal, B. A. (1996) *Trust in Modern Societies*, Cambridge: Polity.

Murphy, J. and Evertson, C. (eds) (1991) *Restructuring Schools: Capturing the Phenomena*, New York: Teachers' College Record.

Murphy, L. R. and Hurrell, J. J. (1987) 'Stress management in the process of occupational stress reduction', *Journal of Managerial Psychology*, 2: 18–23.

Nash, P. (2000) 'Teachers' Benevolent Fund: the teacher support network', paper presented at *Managing Stress in Schools: Teacherline 1st Report Conference*, London, May.

National Governors' Association (1989) *Results in Education*, Washington: NGA.

Newton, T. with Handy, J. and Fineman, S. (1995) *'Managing' Stress: Emotion and Power at Work*, London: Sage.

Nias, J. (1980) 'Commitment and motivation in primary teachers', *Education Review* 33: 181–90.

Nias, J. (1987) 'One finger one thumb: A case study of the deputy head's part in the leadership of a nursery/infant school', in Southworth, G. (ed.) *Readings in Primary School Management*, London: Falmer Press.

Nias, J. (1989) *Primary Teachers Talking: a study of teaching as work*, London, Routledge.

Nias, J. (1991) 'Changing times, changing identities: grieving for a lost self', in Burgess, R. G. (ed.) *Educational Research and Evaluation*, London, Falmer Press.

Nias, J. (1995) 'Teachers' moral purposes: sources of vulnerability and strength', paper presented at Conference on *Teacher Burnout*, Marbach, Germany.

Nias, J. (1996) 'Thinking about feeling: the emotions in teaching', *Cambridge Journal of Education*, 26(3): 293–323.

Nias, J., Southworth, G. and Yeomans, R. (1989) *Staff Relationships in the Primary School*, London: Cassell.

Nias, J., Southworth, G. and Campbell, P. (1992) *Whole School Curriculum Development in the Primary School*, London: Falmer Press.

Offe, C. (1990) 'Reflections on the institutional self-transformation of movement politics, a tentative stage model', in Dalton, J. D. and Kuechler, M. (eds) *Challenging the Political Order: New Socialism and Political Movements in Western Democracies*, Cambridge, Polity Press.

Ofsted (1994) *Primary Matters: A Discussion on Teaching and Learning in Primary Schools*, London: Ofsted.

Ofsted (1995) *The Handbook for the Inspection of Nursery and Primary Schools*, London: Ofsted.

Ofsted (1999) *Lessons Learned from Special Measures: A Report from the Office of Her Majesty's Chief Inspector of Schools*, London: Ofsted.

Office for Standards in Inspection (Ofstin) (1997) *A Better System of Inspection*, Hexham, Northumberland: Ofstin.

O'Grady, C. (1995) 'Growing old together', *The Times Educational Supplement, Primary Forum*, 20 January: 6.

O'Leary, J. (2000) 'School bullying "could cost millions"', *The Times*, 4 January: 7.

Ozga, J. and Lawn, M. (1981) *Teachers Professionalism and Class*, London: Falmer Press.

Parkes, K. R. and Sparkes, T. J. (1998) *Organizational Interventions to Reduce Work Stress: Are They Effective?*, Norwich: Health and Safety Executive.

Pearlin, L. I. (1989) 'The Sociological Study of Stress', *Journal of Health and Social Behaviour*, 30: 241–56.

Pichardo, N. A. (1997) 'New social movements: A critical review', *Annual Review of Sociology*, 23: 411–30.

Pollard, A. (1982) 'A model of classroom coping strategies', *British Journal of Sociology of Education*, 3(1): 19–37.

Pollard, A. (1985) *The Social World of the Primary School*, London: Holt, Rinehart & Winston.

Pollard, A., Broadfoot, P., Croll, P., Osborn, M. and Abbot, D. (1994) *Changing English Primary Schools: The Impact of the Education Reform Act at Key Stage One*, London: Cassell.

Power, M. (1994) *The Audit Explosion*, London: Demos.

Rea, J. and Weiner, G. (1998) 'Cultures of blame and redemption – when empowerment becomes control: practitioners' views of the effective schools movement', in Slee, R. and Weiner, G. with Tomlinson, S. (eds) *School Effectiveness for Whom?*, London: Falmer.

Reay, D. (1996) 'Micro-politics in the 1990s: Staff relationships in secondary schooling', paper presented at the *British Educational Research Association* Conference, University of Lancaster, September.

Relf, S. and Hobbs, D. (1999) 'The recruitment and selection of new teachers of mathematics: the needs of secondary schools versus the teacher training agenda', *Research Papers in Education*, 14(2): 165–80.

Retallick, J., Cocklin, B. and Coombe, K. (eds) (1999) *Learning Communities in Education: Issues and Contexts*, London, Routledge,

Revell, P. (2000) 'Slaying the two-headed hydra of absence', *The Times Educational Supplement, Briefing*, 4 February: 28.

Reynolds, D., Sammons, P., Stoll, L., Barber, M. and Hillman, J. (1996) 'School effectiveness and school improvement in the United Kingdom', *School Effectiveness and School Improvement*, 7(2): 133–58.

Riseborough, G. F. (1981) 'Teacher careers and comprehensive schooling: an empirical study', *Sociology*, 15(3): 352–81.

Rosenholtz, S. J. (1989) 'Workplace conditions that affect teacher quality and commitment: Implications for teacher induction programs', *The Elementary School Journal*, 89(4): 420–39.

Rucht, D. (1990) 'The strategies and action repertoires of new movements' in Dalton, J. D. and Kuechler, M. (eds) *Challenging the Political Order: New Social and Political Movements in Western Democracies*, Cambridge, Cambridge University Press.

Rudow, B. (1999) 'Stress and burnout in the teaching profession: European studies, issues, and research perspectives', in Vandenberghe, R. and Huberman, A. M. (eds) *Understanding and Preventing Teacher Burnout*, Cambridge, Cambridge University Press.

Rutter, M., Maugham, B., Mortimore, P. and Ouston, J. (1979) *Fifteen Thousand Hours*, London: Open Books.

Scanlon, M. (1999) *The Impact of Ofsted Inspections*, Slough: National Foundation for Educational Research.

Schwarzer, R. and Greenglass, E. (1999) 'Teacher burnout from a social-cognitive perspective: A theoretical position paper', in Vandenberghe, R. and Huberman, A. M. (eds) *Understanding and Preventing Teacher Burnout*, Cambridge, Cambridge University Press.

Sears, N. (1998) 'Teachers' spouses have their grouses', *The Times Educational Supplement*, 30 January: 4.

Seddon, T. (1991) 'Restructuring teachers and teaching: Current Australian developments and future prospects', *Discourse*, 12(1): 1–23.

Sennett, R. (1998) *The Corrosion of Character: The Personal Consequences of Work in the New Capitalism*, New York and London: Norton.

Sergiovanni, T. J. (1999) 'Conflicting mindscapes and the inevitability of stress in teaching', in Vandenberghe, R. and Huberman, A. M. (eds) *Understanding and Preventing Teacher Burnout*, Cambridge, Cambridge University Press.

Shilling, C. (1992) 'Reconceptualising structure and agency in the sociology of education: structuration theory and schooling', *British Journal of Sociology of Education*, 3(1): 69–88.

Sikes, P., Measor, L. and Woods, P. (1985) *Teacher Careers: Crises and Continuities*, Lewes: Falmer Press.

Slater, J. (2000) 'The Great Escape', *The Times Educational Supplement, Briefing*, January, 28: 30.

Slee, R. and Weiner, G. with Tomlinson, S. (eds) (1998) *School Effectiveness for Whom?*, London: Falmer.

Sleegers, P. (1999) 'Professional identity, school reform, and burnout: Some reflections on teacher burnout', in Vandenberghe, R. and Huberman, A. M. (eds) *Understanding and Preventing Teacher Burnout*, Cambridge, Cambridge University Press.

Smithers, A. (1989) 'Where have all the teachers gone?', *The Times Educational Supplement*, 12 May: 17.

Smylie, M. A. (1995) 'Teacher stress in a time of reform', paper presented at conference on *Teacher Burnout*, Marbach, November.

Smylie, M. (1999) 'Teacher stress in a time of reform', in Vandenberghe, R. and Huberman, A. M. *Understanding and Preventing Teacher Burnout*, Cambridge: Cambridge University Press.

Smyth, J. (1991) 'International perspectives on teacher collegiality: a labour process discussion based on the concept of teachers' work', *British Journal of Sociology of Education*, 12(3): 323–46.

Snow, D. A. and Anderson, L. (1987) 'Identity work among the homeless: The verbal construction and avowal of personal identities', *American Journal of Sociology*, 92(6): 1336–71.

Stoll, L. and Myers, K. (eds) (1998) *No Quick Fixes: Perspectives on Schools in Difficulty*, London: Falmer Press.

Stone, S. (1997) 'The pill and the pendulum', *The Guardian*, G2, 9 December: 15.

Strauss, A. L. (1971) *Professions, Work and Careers*, San Francisco: The Sociology Press.

Sutherland, S. (1997) 'Teacher education and training: a study', an appendix to *The Dearing Report*, London: HMSO.

Taylor, V. (1998) 'Feminist methodology in social movements research', *Qualitative Sociology* 21: 357–80.

Teacher Training Agency (1997) *National Standards for Headteachers*, London: TTA.

Thomas, N. (1990) *Primary Education from Plowden to the 1990s*, Basingstoke: Falmer Press.

Thornton, M. (1999) 'Reducing wastage among men student teachers in primary courses: a male club approach', *Journal of Education for Teaching*, 25(1): 41–53.

Tickle, L. (1999) 'Teacher induction: Limits and possibilities', paper presented at the *British Educational Research Association* Conference, University of Sussex, September.

Times Educational Supplement, The (2000) 'They're all out to get me . . .' First Appointments, 14 January: 14.

Travers, C. J. and Cooper, C. (1996) *Teachers Under Pressure: Stress in the Teaching Profession*, London: Routledge.

Troman, G. (1997) 'The effects of restructuring on primary teachers' work: A sociological analysis', unpublished PhD thesis, The Open University.

Troman, G. (1999) 'Experiencing naming, blaming and shaming: Teacher stress in a "failing" school', paper presented at the *British Educational Research Association* Conference, University of Sussex, September.

Troman, G. (2000a) 'Teacher stress in the low-trust society', *British Journal of Sociology of Education*, 21(3): 331–53.

Troman, G. (2000b) 'Trusting in teamwork: The low-stress school', paper presented at the *European Educational Research Association* Conference, University of Edinburgh, September.

Troman, G. and Woods, P. (2000) 'Careers under stress: Teacher adaptations at a time of intensive reform', *Journal of Educational Change*, 1(3): 1–23.

Vandenberghe, R. and Huberman, A. M. (eds) (1999) *Understanding and Preventing Teacher Burnout*, Cambridge: Cambridge University Press.

Vulliamy, G. and Webb, R. (1991) 'Teacher research and educational change: an empirical study', *British Educational Research Journal*, 17(3): 219–36.

Walker, S. and Barton, L. (eds) (1987) *Changing Policies, Changing Teachers*, Milton Keynes: Open University Press.

Webb, R. and Vulliamy, G. (1996) *Roles and Responsibilities in the Primary School: Changing Demands, Changing Practices*, Buckingham: Open University Press.

Weber, M. (1947) *The Theory of Social and Economic Organization*, trans. Henderson, A. M. and Parsons, T., Oxford: Oxford University Press.

Whitehead, M. (1996) 'The drip-drip-drip despair that slowly destroys lives', *The Times Educational Supplement, School Management Update*, 10 May: 6.

Wilcox, B. and Gray, J. (1996) *Inspecting Schools: Holding Schools to Account and Helping Schools to Improve*, Buckingham, Open University Press.

Willmott, R. (1999a) 'Structure, agency and school effectiveness: researching a 'failing' school', *Educational Studies*, 25(1): 5–18.

Willmott, R. (1999b) 'Structure, agency and the sociology of education: rescuing analytical dualism', *British Journal of Sociology of Education*, 20(1): 5–21.

Wolpert, L. (1999) *Malignant Sadness: The Anatomy of Depression*, London: Faber & Faber.

Woodham, A. (1995) *Beating Stress at Work*, London: Health Education Authority.

Woodhead, C. (1995) *A Question of Standards: Finding the Balance*, London: Politea.

Woods, P. (1979) *The Divided School*, London: Routledge & Kegan Paul.

Woods, P. (1981) 'Strategies, commitment and identity: making and breaking the teacher role', in Barton, L. and Walker, S. (eds) *Schools, Teachers and Teaching*, Lewes: Falmer Press.

Woods, P. (1983) *Sociology and the School: An Interactionist Viewpoint*, London: Routledge & Kegan Paul.

Woods, P. (1990) *Teacher Skills and Strategies*, Buckingham: Open University Press.

Woods, P. (1995a) 'The intensification of the teacher's self', paper presented at the *Conference on Teacher Burnout*, Marbach, November.

Woods, P. (1995b) *Creative Teachers in Primary Schools*, Buckingham: Open University Press.

Woods, P. (1996a) 'Primary Teacher Stress and Burnout', research proposal submitted to the Economic and Social Research Council.

Woods, P. (1996b) *Researching the Art of Teaching: Ethnography for Educational Use*, London: Routledge.

Woods, P. (1999a) 'Teaching and learning in the new millennium', keynote address given at *Malaysian Educational Research Association* Conference *(MERA)*, Malacca, 1–3 December.

Woods, P. (1999b) 'Talking about Coombes: Features of a learning community', in Retallick, J., Cocklin, B. and Coombe, K. (eds) *Learning Communities in Education*, London: Routledge.

Woods, P. and Jeffrey, R. J. (1996) *Teachable Moments: The Art of Teaching in Primary Schools*, Buckingham: Open University Press.

Woods, P., Jeffrey, B., Troman, G. and Boyle, M. (1997) *Restructuring Schools; Reconstructing Teachers: Responding To Change In The Primary School*, Buckingham: Open University Press.

Woods, P., Jeffrey, B. and Troman G. (2000) 'The Impact of New Labour's Educational Policy on Primary Schools', in Fielding, M. (ed.) *Taking Education Really Seriously: Three Years' Hard Labour*, (forthcoming).

Woodward, W. (2000) 'Teachers' sick leave adds up to 2.5 million days lost', *The Guardian*, 13 May: 7.

Wragg, E. C., Wragg, C. M., Haynes, G. S and Chamberlin, R. P. (1998) *Teaching Competence Project, Occasional Paper 1*, Exeter: University of Exeter School of Education.

Young, S. (1997) 'Recruitment crisis looms', *The Times Educational Supplement*, 2 May: 7.

Author index

Subject index